THE WHOLENESS OF LIFE

Born near Madras, Jiddu Krishnamurti (1895–1986) was fourteen when he was taken under the guardianship of Mrs Annie Besant, socialist, reformer and President of the International Theosophical Society at Adyar, near Madras. She and her colleague, C. W. Leadbeater, believed that Krishnamurti was the vehicle for the Messiah whose coming the Theosophists had predicted. The Order of the Star in the East, an organisation dedicated to preparing mankind for the coming of the World Teacher, was formed in 1911 with Krishnamurti at its head. In the same year he was brought to England to be privately educated and trained for his coming role. In 1929, however, he dissolved the order and relinquished the money and property which had accumulated in his name. He declared that truth cannot be found through any sect or religion but only by freeing oneself from all forms of conditioning. "You can form other organisations and expect someone else," he said. "With that I am not concerned, nor with creating new cages ... My only concern is to set men absolutely, unconditionally free."

Long recognised as one of the world's foremost spiritual teachers, Krishnamurti dedicated his life to speaking throughout the world. Staying nowhere for more than a few months at a time, he did not consider himself as belonging to any race or country. Over the years, his annual gatherings in India, at Ojai, California, at Saanen in Switzerland and at Brockwood Park in Hampshire attracted thousands of people of different nationality, occupation and outlook.

BOOKS BY KRISHNAMURTI PUBLISHED BY GOLLANCZ:

THE FIRST AND LAST FREEDOM

EDUCATION AND THE SIGNIFICANCE OF LIFE

COMMENTARIES ON LIVING: FIRST SERIES

COMMENTARIES ON LIVING: SECOND SERIES

COMMENTARIES ON LIVING: THIRD SERIES

LIFE AHEAD

THIS MATTER OF CULTURE

FREEDOM FROM THE KNOWN

THE ONLY REVOLUTION

THE URGENCY OF CHANGE

THE IMPOSSIBLE QUESTION

BEYOND VIOLENCE

THE AWAKENING OF INTELLIGENCE

BEGINNINGS OF LEARNING

KRISHNAMURTI'S NOTEBOOK

TRUTH AND ACTUALITY

THE WHOLENESS OF LIFE

EXPLORATION INTO INSIGHT

MEDITATIONS

POEMS AND PARABLES

KRISHNAMURTI'S JOURNAL

THE ENDING OF TIME
(with Dr David Bohm)

LAST TALKS AT SAANEN 1985
(illustrated with photographs)

KRISHNAMURTI TO HIMSELF

THE FUTURE IS NOW

THE WHOLENESS OF LIFE

by

KRISHNAMURTI

LONDON
VICTOR GOLLANCZ LTD
1991

First published in Great Britain 1978
by Victor Gollancz Ltd,
14 Henrietta Street, London WC2E 8QJ

First published in paperback 1983

Gollancz Paperback edition first published November 1985
Second impression April 1988

This edition first published 1991

British Library Cataloguing in Publication Data
Krishnamurti, J.
    The wholeness of life.
    1. Life
    I. Title
    128'.5   BD435
    ISBN 0-575-03371-1

Printed in Finland by Werner Södeström Oy

CONTENTS

Part I
Seven Dialogues

Abridged discussions between Krishnamurti, Dr David Bohm, Professor of Theoretical Physics at Birkbeck College, University of London, and Dr David Shainberg, a Psychiatrist of New York City. (Abridged from video-tape recordings at Brockwood Park, Hampshire, in May 1976.)

Dialogue I	9
Dialogue II	26
Dialogue III	48
Dialogue IV	62
Dialogue V	79
Dialogue VI	99
Dialogue VII	117

Part II
The substance of the public talks given in Ojai, California; Saanen, Switzerland; and Brockwood Park, England, during 1977.

I	Meditation is the emptying of the content of consciousness	141
II	The end of conflict is the gathering of supreme energy which is a form of intelligence	146
III	Out of negation comes the positive called love	150
IV	Death—a great act of purgation	154
V	Action which is skilful and which does not perpetuate the self	156
VI	Reason and logic alone will not discover truth	159
VII	Intelligence, in which there is complete security	163
VIII	In negation the positive is born	167
IX	Because there is space, there is emptiness and total silence	173

X   The state of the mind that has insight is completely
      empty   177

XI   Where there is suffering you cannot possibly love   181

XII   Sorrow is the outcome of time and thought   183

XIII What is death?   189

XIV   That emptiness is the summation of all energy   192

XV   When the 'me' is not, then compassion comes into
      being   198

XVI   The division between the observer and the
      observed is the source of conflict   202

XVII When there is an ending to consciousness with its
      content there is something entirely different   207

XVIII Without clarity, skill becomes a most dangerous
      thing   212

XIX   How is one to know oneself?   215

Part III
Two Dialogues

Krishnamurti talks with a small group at Ojai drawn from the Krishnamurti schools and Foundations in Canada, England, India and USA.

Dialogue I   221
Dialogue II   233

DIALOGUE I

May 17

KRISHNAMURTI: Can we talk about the wholeness of life? Can one be aware of that wholeness if the mind is fragmented? You can't be aware of the whole if you are only looking through a small hole.

Dr Shainberg: Right. But on the other hand in actuality you are the whole.

K: Ah! That is theory.

S: Is it?

Dr Bohm: A supposition, of course it is.

K: Of course, when you are fragmented how can you assume that you are the whole?

S: How am I to know I am fragmented?

K: When there is conflict.

S: That's right.

K: When opposing desires, opposing wishes, opposing thoughts bring conflict. Then you have pain, then you become conscious of your fragmentation.

S: Right. But at those moments it often happens that you don't want to let go of the conflict.

K: That is a different matter. What we are asking is: Can the fragment dissolve itself, for then only it is possible to see the whole.

S: All you really know is your fragmentation.

K: That is all we know.

B: That is right.

K: Therefore let's stick to that.

B: The supposition that there is a whole may be reasonable but as long as you are fragmented you could never see it. It would be just an assumption.

K: Of course, right.

S: Right.

B: You may think you have experienced it once, but that is also an assumption.

K: Absolutely. Quite right.

S: You know, I wonder if there is not a tremendous pain or something that goes on when I am aware of my fragmentation—a loneliness somehow.

K: Look, sir: Can you be aware of your fragment? That you are an American, that I am a Hindu, Jew, Communist or whatever—you just live in that state. You don't say, "Well I know I am a Hindu"—it is only when you are challenged, it is only when it is said, "What are you?" that you say, "I am an Indian, or a Hindu, or an Arab".

B: When the country is challenged then you have got to worry.

K: Of course.

S: So you are saying that I am living totally reactively?

K: No, you are living totally in a kind of miasma, confusion.

S: From one piece to the next, from one reaction to the next reaction.

K: So can we be aware, actually, of the various fragments? That I am a Hindu, that I am a Jew, that I am an Arab, that I am a Communist, that I am a Catholic, that I am a businessman, that I am married, that I have responsibilities; I am an artist, I am a scientist—you follow? All this sociological fragmentation.

S: Right.

K: As well as psychological fragmentation.

S: Right, right. That is exactly what I started with. This feeling that I am a fragment.

K: Which you call the individual.

S: That I call important, not just the individual.

K: You call that important.

S: Right. That I have to work.

K: Quite.

S: It is significant.

10

K: So can we now, in talking together, be aware that I am that? I am a fragment and therefore creating more fragments, more conflict, more misery, more confusion, more sorrow, because when there is conflict it affects everything.

S: Right.

K: Can you be aware of it as we are discussing?

S: I can be aware a little as we are discussing.

K: Not a little.

S: That's the trouble. Why can't I be aware of it?

K: Look, sir. You are only aware of it when there is conflict. It is not a conflict in you now.

B: But is it possible to be aware of it without conflict?

K: That is the next thing, yes. That requires quite a different approach.

B: But I was thinking of looking at one point—that the importance of these fragments is that when I identify myself and say "I am this", "I am that", I mean the whole of me. The whole of me is rich or poor, or American, or whatever, and therefore it seems all-important. I think the trouble is that the fragment claims it is the whole, and makes itself very important.

S: Takes up the whole life.

B: Then comes a contradiction, and then comes another fragment saying it is the whole.

K: You know this whole world is broken up that way, outside and inside.

S: Me and you.

K: Yes, me and you, we and they . . .

B: But if we say "I am wholly this", then we also say "I am wholly that".

S: This movement into fragmentation almost seems to be caused by something. It seems to be . . .

K: Is this what you are asking? What is the cause of this fragmentation?

S: Yes. What is the cause of the fragmentation? What breeds it? What sucks us into it?

K: We are asking something very important, which is: What is the cause of this fragmentation?

S: That is what I was getting into. There is some cause . . . I have got to hold on to something.

K: No. Just look at it, sir. Why are you fragmented?

S: Well, my immediate response is the need to hold on to something.

K: No, much deeper than that. Much deeper. Look at it. Look at it. Let's go slowly into it.

S: OK.

K: Not immediate responses. What brings this conflict which indicates I am fragmented, and then I ask the question: What brings this fragmentation? What is the cause of it?

B: Right. That is important.

K: Yes. Why are you and I and the majority of the world fragmented? What is the cause of it?

B: It seems we won't find the cause by going back in time to a certain . . .

S: I am not looking for genetics, I am looking for right this second . . .

K: Sir, just look at it. Put it on the table and look at it objectively. What brings about this fragmentation?

S: Fear.

K: No, no, much more.

B: Maybe the fragmentation causes fear.

K: Yes, that's it. Why am I a Hindu?—if I am, I am not a Hindu, I am not an Indian, I have no nationality. But suppose I call myself a Hindu. What makes me a Hindu?

S: Well, conditioning makes you a Hindu.

K: What is the background, what is it that makes me say "I am a Hindu"? Which is a fragmentation, obviously.

S: Right, right.

K: What makes it? My father, my grandfather—generations and generations before me, 10,000 or 5,000 years, they have been saying you are a Brahmin.

12

S: You don't say or write I am a Brahmin, you are a Brahmin. Right? That is quite different. You say I am a Brahmin because . . .

K: It is like you saying I am a Christian. Which is what?

S: Tradition, conditioning, sociology, history, culture, family, everything.

K: But behind that, what is behind that?

S: Behind that is man's . . .

K: No, no. Don't theorize. Look at it in yourself.

S: Well, it gives me a place, an identity; I know who I am then, I have my little niche.

K: Who made that niche?

S: Well, I made it and they helped me make it. I am co-operating in this very . . .

K: You are not co-operating. You *are* it.

S: I am it. Right. That's right. The whole thing is moving towards . . . putting me in a hole.

K: So what made you? The great-great-grandparent created this environment, this culture, this whole structure of human existence, with all its misery, all its conflict—which is the fragmentation.

S: The same action that makes man right now.

K: Exactly. The Babylonians, the Egyptians, we are exactly the same now.

B: Yes.

S: This is all giving me my second-hand existence.

K: Yes. Proceed. Let's go into it. Let's find out why man has brought about this state. Which we accept—you follow? Gladly or unwillingly, we are of it. I am willing to kill somebody because he is a Communist or a Fascist, an Arab or a Jew, a Protestant or a Catholic or whatever it is.

S: Well, everywhere, the doctors, laywers . . .

K: Of course, of course. The same problem. Is it the desire for security? Biological as well as psychological security?

S: You could say yes.

13

K: If I belong to something, to some organization, to some group, to some sect, to some ideological community, I am safe there.

B: That is not clear: you may feel safe.

K: I feel safe then. But it may not be safety.

B: Yes, But why don't I see that I am not really safe?

K: Go into it.

S: I don't see it.

K: Just look. I join a community . . .

S: Right. I am a doctor.

K: Yes, you are a doctor.

S: I get all these ideas. . . .

K: Because you are a doctor you have a special position in society.

S: Right. I have a lot of ideas of how things work.

K: You are in a special position in society and therefore you are completely safe.

S: Right.

K: You can malpractice, but you are very protected by other doctors, other organizations—you follow?

S: Right.

K: You feel secure.

B: It is essential that I shouldn't enquire too far to feel secure, isn't it? In other words I must stop my enquiry at a certain point. If I start to ask too many questions . . .

K: . . . then you are out! If I begin to ask questions about my community and my relation to that community, my relationship to the world, my relation to my neighbour, I am finished. I am out of the community. I am lost.

S: That's right.

K: So to feel safe, secure, protected, I belong.

S: I depend.

K: I depend.

B: I depend wholly in one sense that if I don't have that, then I feel the whole thing is sunk.

14

S: You see, not only do I depend but every problem I now have is with reference to this dependency. I don't know about the patient, I only know how the patient doesn't fit into my system.

K: Quite, quite.

S: Because that is my conflict.

K: He is your victim.

S: That's right, my victim.

B: You see, as long as I don't ask questions I can feel comfortable. But I feel uncomfortable when I do ask questions, very deeply uncomfortable. Because the whole of my situation is challenged. But then if I look at it more broadly I see the whole thing has no foundation—it is all dangerous. This community itself is in a mess, it may collapse. Even if the whole of it doesn't collapse, you can't count on the academic profession any more, they may not give money for universities. Everything is changing so fast that you don't know where you are. So why should I go on with not asking questions?

K: Why don't I ask questions?—Because of fear.

B: Yes, but that fear is from fragmentations.

K: Of course. So is that the beginning of this fragmentation? Does fragmentation take place when one is seeking security?

S: But why . . .?

K: Both biologically as well as psychologically. Primarily psychologically, then biologically.

S: Right.

K: Physically.

B: But isn't the tendency to seek physical security built into the organism?

K: Yes, that's right. It is. I must have food, clothes, shelter. It is absolutely necessary.

S: Right.

K: And when that is threatened—if I questioned the Communist system altogether, living in Russia, I am a non person.

S: But let's go a little bit slower here. You are suggesting that in my need for security, biologically, I must have some fragmentation.

15

K: No, sir. Biologically, fragmentation takes place, the insecurity takes place, when psychologically I want security.

S: OK.

K: I don't know if I am making myself clear. Wait a minute. That is: if I don't psychologically belong to a group, then I am out of that group.

S: Then I am insecure.

K: I am insecure, and because the group gives me security, physical security, I accept everything they give me.

S: Right.

K: But the moment I object psychologically to the structure of the society and the community I am lost. This is an obvious fact.

S: Right.

B: Yes.

S: Were you suggesting then that the basic insecurity we live in is being conditioned, and the response to this—the answer to this—is a conditioned fragmentation?

K: Partly.

S: And that the movement of fragmentation is the conditioning?

K: Sir, look: if there were no fragmentation, historically, geographically, nationally, we would live perfectly safely. We would all be protected, we would all have food, all have houses. There would be no wars, we'd be all one. He is my brother, I am him. He is me. But this fragmentation prevents that taking place.

S: Right. So you are suggesting even more there—you are suggesting that we would help each other?

K: I would help, obviously.

B: We are going round in a circle because . . .

K: Yes, sir, I want to get back to something, which is: if there were no nationalities, no ideological groups, and so on, we would have everything we want. That is prevented because I am a Hindu, you are an Arab, he is a Russian—you follow? We are asking: Why does this fragmentation take place? What is the source of it? Is it knowledge?

S: It is knowledge, you say.

K: Is it knowledge? I am sure it is, but I am putting it as a question.

S: It certainly seems to be.

K: No, no. Look into it. Let's find out.

S: What do you mean by knowledge, what are you talking about there?

K: The word to know. Do I know you? Or have I known you? I can never say I know you, I mean actually; it would be an abomination to say "I know you". I have known you. But you in the meantime are changing—there is a great deal of movement going on in you.

S: Right.

K: To say I know you means I am acquainted or intimate with that movement which is going on in you. It would be impudence on my part to say I know you.

S: That's right.

K: So knowing—to know—is the past. Would you say that?

B: Yes, I mean what we know is the past.

K: Knowledge is the past.

B: The danger is that we call it the present. The danger is that we call knowledge the present.

K: That is just it.

B: In other words, if we said the past is the past, then wouldn't you say it needn't fragment?

K: What is that, sir?

B: If we said—if we recognized, acknowledged, that the past is the past, that it is gone, and therefore what we know is the past, then it would not introduce fragmentation.

K: No, it wouldn't, quite right.

B: But if we say what we know is what is present now, then we are introducing fragmentation.

K: Quite right.

B: Because we are imposing this partial knowledge on the whole.

K: Sir, would you say knowledge is one of the factors of fragmentation? It is a large pill to swallow!

17

B: And also there are plenty of other factors.

K: Yes. But that may be the only factor!

B: I think we should look at it this way, that people hope through knowledge to overcome fragmentation.

K: Of course.

B: To produce a system of knowledge that will put it all together.

K: Is that not one of the major factors, or perhaps *the* factor of fragmentation? My experience tells me I am a Hindu: my experience tells me that I know what god is.

B: Wouldn't we better say that confusion about the whole of knowledge is because of fragmentation?

K: That is what we were saying the other day—art is putting things in their right place. So I will put knowledge in its right place.

B: Yes, so that we are not confused about it.

K: Of course.

S: You know I was just going to read you this rather interesting example of a patient of mine who was teaching me something the other day. She said, "I have the feeling that the way you doctors operate is that you have certain kinds of patients, and if you do 'x' to them you will get a certain kind of effect. You are not talking to me, you are doing this to me hoping you will get this result."

K: Quite.

S: That is what you are saying.

K: No, a little more, sir, than that. We are saying, both Dr Bohm and I, we are saying that knowledge has its place.

S: Let's go into that.

K: Like driving a car, learning a language and so on.

B: If we drive a car using knowledge, that is not fragmentation.

K: No, but when knowledge is used psychologically . . .

B: One should see more clearly what the difference is. The car itself—as I see it—is a part, a limited part, that can be handled by knowledge.

S: It is a limited part of life.

18

B: Of life, yes. When we say, I am so and so, I mean the whole of me. And therefore I am applying the part to the whole. I am trying to take in the whole by the part.

K: When knowledge assumes it understands the whole . . .

B: But it is often very tricky because I am not explicitly spelling out that I understand the whole, but it is implicit by saying I, or everything, is this way.

K: Quite, quite.

B: It implies that the whole is this way, you see. The whole of me, the whole of life, the whole of the world.

S: As Krishnaji was saying about never knowing a person—that is how we deal with ourselves. We say I know this and that about myself rather than being open to the new man. Or even being aware of the fragmentation.

B: If I am talking about you then I shouldn't say I know all because you are not a limited part like a machine. You see, the machine is fairly limited and you can know all that is relevant about it, or most of it anyway. Sometimes it breaks down.

K: Quite. Quite.

B: But when it comes to another person, that is immensely beyond what you could really know. The past experience doesn't tell you the essence.

K: Are you saying, Dr Bohm, that when knowledge spills over into the psychological field . . .?

B: Well, also in another field which I call the whole in general. Sometimes it spills over into the philosophical field and then tries to make it metaphysical, the whole universe.

K: That is purely theoretical and has no meaning for me personally.

B: I mean that some people feel that when they are discussing metaphysics of the whole universe it is not psychological. It probably is, but some people may feel that they are making a theory of the universe, not discussing psychology. It is just a matter of language.

K: Language, quite.

S: Well you see what you are saying can be extended to what

19

people are. They have a metaphysics about other people. I know all other people are not to be trusted.

K: Of course.

B: You have a metaphysics about yourself, saying I am such and such a person.

S: Right. I have a metaphysics that life is hopeless and I must depend on these things.

K: No, all that you can see is that we are fragmented. That is a fact. And I am aware of those fragmentations; there is an awareness of the fragmented mind because of conflict.

S: That's right.

B: You were saying before that we have got to have an approach where we are not aware of the fragmented mind just because of conflict.

K: Yes. That's right.

B: Are we coming to that?

K: Coming, yes. I said: What is the source of this conflict? The source is fragmentation, obviously. What brings about fragmentation? What is the cause of it? What is behind it? We said perhaps knowledge.

S: Knowledge.

K: Knowledge. Psychologically I use knowledge; I think I know myself, when I really don't, because I am changing, moving. Or I use knowledge for my own satisfaction—for my position, for my success, for becoming a great man in the world. I am a great scholar, say. I have read a million books. This gives me position, prestige, a status. So is that it—that fragmentation takes place when there is a desire for security, psychological security, which prevents biological security?

S: Right.

K: You say right. Therefore security may be one of the factors. Security in knowledge, used wrongly.

B: Or could you say that some sort of mistake has been made, that man feels insecure biologically, and he thinks, what shall I do, and he makes a mistake in the sense that he tries to obtain a psychological sense of security—by knowledge?

K: By knowledge, yes.

S: By knowing, yes. By repeating himself, by depending on all these structures.

K: One feels secure by having an ideal.

S: Right. That is so true.

B: But somewhere one asks why the person makes this mistake. In other words if thought—if the mind had been absolutely clear, it would never have done that.

S: If the mind had been absolutely clear—but we have just said that there is biological insecurity. That is a fact.

B: But that doesn't imply that you have to delude yourself.

K: Quite right. Go on further.

S: There's that biological fact of my constant uncertainty. The biological fact of constant change.

K: That is created through psychological fragmentation.

S: My biological uncertainty?

K: Of course. I may lose my job, I may have no money tomorrow.

B: Now let's look at that. I may have no money tomorrow. You see, that may be an actual fact, but now the question is: What would a man say if his mind were clear, what would be his response?

K: He would never be put in that position.

S: He wouldn't ask that question.

B: But suppose he finds himself without money?

K: He would do something.

B: His mind won't just go to pieces.

S: He won't have to have all the money he thinks he has to have.

B: Besides that, he won't go into this well of confusion.

K: No, absolutely.

S: The problem 99 per cent of the time, I certainly agree, is that we all think we need more than this ideal of what we should have.

K: No, sir. We are trying to stick to one point. What is the cause of this fragmentation?

21

S: Right.

K: We said knowledge spilling over into the field where it should not enter.

B: But why does it do so?

K: Why does it do so? That is fairly simple.

S: My sense of it from what we have been saying is that it does so in the illusion of security. Thought creates the illusion that there is security.

B: Yes, but why doesn't intelligence show that there is no security?

S: Why doesn't intelligence show it?

K: Can a fragmented mind be intelligent?

S: No.

B: Well, it resists intelligence.

K: It can pretend to be intelligent.

B: Yes. But are you saying that once the mind fragments then intelligence is gone?

K: Yes.

B: But now you are querying this problem. You are also saying that there can be an end to fragmentation.

K: That's right.

B: That would seem to be a contradiction.

K: It looks like that but it is not.

S: All I know is fragmentation.

K: Therefore . . .

S: That is what I have got.

K: Let's stick to it and prove it can end. Go through it.

B: But if you say intelligence cannot operate when the mind is fragmented . . .

K: Is psychological security more important than biological security?

S: That is an interesting question.

K: Go on.

S: One thing we have condensed . . .

K: No, I am asking. Don't move away from the question. I am asking: Is psychological security more important than biological security, physical security?

S: It isn't but it sounds like it is.

K: No, don't move away from it. I am asking. Stick to it. Is it to you?

S: I would say yes, psychological seems . . .

B: What is actually true?

S: Actually true, no. Biological security is more important.

K: Biological? Are you sure?

S: No. I think psychological security is what I actually worry about most.

K: Psychological security.

S: That is what I worry about most.

K: Which prevents biological security.

S: Right. I've figured that one out now.

K: No, no. Because I am seeking psychological security in ideas, in knowledge, in images, in confusions, this prevents me from having biological, physical security—for myself, for my children, for my brothers. I can't have it. Because psychological security says I am a Hindu, a blasted somebody in a little corner.

S: No question. I do feel that psychological . . .

K: So can we be free of the desire to be psychologically secure?

S: That's right. That is the question.

K: Of course it is.

S: That's the nub of it, right.

K: Last night I was listening to some people arguing on television—the chairman of this, the something of that, talking about Ireland, and various other things. Each man was completely convinced of what he was saying.

S: That's right. I am sitting on meetings every week. Each man thinks his category is the most important.

23

K: So man has given more importance to psychological security than to biological, physical security.

B: But it is not clear why he should delude himself in this way.

K: He has deluded himself because—why, why?

S: Images, power.

K: No, sir, it is much deeper than that. Why has he given importance to psychological security?

S: We seem to think that that is where security is.

K: No. Look more into it. The me is the most important thing.

S: Right. That is the same thing.

K: No, me. My position, my happiness, my money, my house, my wife—me.

B: Me. Yes. And isn't it that each person feels he is the essence of the whole? The me is the very essence of the whole. I would feel if the me were gone that the rest wouldn't mean anything.

K: That is the whole point. The me gives me complete security, psychologically.

B: It seems all-important. Of course.

S: All-important.

B: Yes, people say if I am sad then the whole world has no meaning—right?

S: It is not only that; I am sad if the me is all-important.

K: No. We are saying that in the me is the greatest security.

S: Right. That is what we think.

K: No. Not we think. It is so.

B: What do you mean it is so?

K: In the world that is what is happening.

B: That is what is happening. But it is a delusion.

K: We will come to that later.

S: I think that is a good point. That it is so; that the me—I like that way of getting at it—the me *is* what is important. That is all it is.

K: Psychologically.

S: Psychologically.

K: Me, my country, my god, my house.

S: We have got your point.

DIALOGUE II

May 18—morning

KRISHNAMURTI: May we go on where we left off yesterday? Or would you like to start something new?

Dr Bohm: I thought there was a point that wasn't entirely clear about what we were discussing yesterday. We rather accepted that security, psychological security, was wrong, was a delusion, but in general I don't think we made it very clear why we think it is a delusion. You see, most people feel that psychological security is a good thing and quite necessary, and that when it is disturbed, when a person is frightened, or sorrowful even—so disturbed that he might require treatment—he feels that psychological security is necessary before he can even begin to do anything.

K: Yes, right.

B: I don't think it's at all clear why one should say it is not really as important as physical security.

K: I think we have made it fairly clear but let's go into it. Is there really psychological security at all?

B: I don't think we discussed that fully yesterday.

K: Of course. Nobody accepts that. But we are enquiring into it, going into the problem of it.

B: I think that if you told somebody who was feeling very disturbed mentally that there is no psychological security he would just feel worse.

K: Collapse. Of course.

Dr Shainberg: Right.

K: We are talking of fairly sane, rational people.

S: OK.

K: We are questioning whether there is any psychological security

26

at all. Permanency, stability, a sense of well-founded, deep-rooted existence, psychologically . . . I believe in something . . .

S: . . . and that gives me . . .

K: It may be the most foolish belief . . .

S: Right.

K: . . . a neurotic belief. I believe in it.

S: Right.

K: And that gives me a tremendous sense of vitality and stability.

B: I can think of two examples: one is that if I could really believe that after dying I would go to heaven, make quite sure of it, then I could be very secure anywhere, no matter what happens.

S: That would make you feel good.

B: Well, I wouldn't really have to worry; it would all be a temporary trouble; I would be pretty sure that in time it was all going to be very good. Do you see?

K: Right. That is the whole Asiatic attitude, more or less.

B: Or if I am a Communist, I think that in time Communism is going to solve everything; we are going through a lot of troubles now but it is all going to be worth while, and in the end everything will be all right. If I could be sure of that then I would feel very secure inside, even if conditions are hard now.

S: OK. All right.

K: So although one may have these strong beliefs which give one a sense of security, of permanency, we are questioning whether there is such a thing in reality, in actuality . . .

S: Yes, yes. But I want to ask David something. Take a scientist, a guy who is going to his laboratory every day, or take a doctor—is he getting security from the very routinization of his life?

K: His knowledge.

S: Yes, from his knowledge.

B: Well, he makes believe he is learning the permanent laws of nature, really getting something that means something.

S: Yes.

B: And also getting a position in society—being well known and respected and financially secure.

27

S: He believes that these things will give him security. The mother believes that a child will give her security.

K: Don't you have security psychologically?

S: Yes. I get a security out of my knowledge, out of my routine, out of my patients, out of seeing my patients, out of my position . . .

B: But there is conflict in that because if I think it over a little bit I doubt it, I question it. I say it doesn't look all that secure, anything may happen. There may be a war, there may be a depression, there may be a flood.

S: Right.

K: There may be sane people all of a sudden in the world!

B: So I say there is conflict and confusion in my security because I am not sure about it. But if I had an absolute belief in god and heaven . . .

K: This is so obvious!

S: It is obvious. I agree with you it is obvious but I think it has to be really felt.

K: But, sir, you, Dr Shainberg, you are the victim.

S: I'll be the victim.

K: For the moment. Don't you have strong belief?

S: Right.

K: Don't you have a sense of permanency somewhere inside you?

S: I think I do.

K: Psychologically?

S: Yes, I do. I mean I have a sense of permanency about my intention.

K: Intention?

S: I mean my work.

K: Your knowledge?

S: . . . my knowledge, my . . .

K: . . . status . . .

S: . . . my status, the continuity of my interest. You know what I mean?

K: Yes.

S: There is a sense of security and the feeling that I can help someone.

K: Yes.

S: And that I can do my work.

K: That gives you security, psychological security.

S: There is something about it that is secure. What am I saying when I say "security"? I am saying that I won't be lonely.

K: No, no. Feeling secure. That you have something that is imperishable.

S: Which means—no I don't feel it that way. I feel it more in the sense of what is going to happen in time. What am I going to have to depend on?—what is my time going to be?—am I going to be lonely, is it going to be empty?

K: No, sir.

S: Isn't that security?

K: As Dr Bohm pointed out, if one has a strong belief in reincarnation, as the whole Asiatic world has, then it doesn't matter what happens. You may be miserable this life but next life you will be happier. So that gives you a great sense of "this is unimportant, but that is important".

S: Right, right.

K: And that gives me a sense of great comfort, for this is a transient world anyhow and eventually I will get to something permanent.

S: That is in the Asiatic world; but I think in the Western world you don't have that . . .

K: Oh, yes, you have it.

S: . . . with a different focus.

K: Of course.

B: It is different but we have always had the search for security.

S: Right, right. But what do you think security is? I mean, for instance, you became a scientist, you have your own laboratory, you pick up books all the time—right? What the hell do you call security?

K: Having something . . .

29

S: Knowledge?

K: Something which you can cling to and which is not perishable. It may perish eventually but for the time being, it is there to hold on to.

B: You feel that it is permanent. Like people in the past who used to accumulate gold because gold is the symbol of the imperishable.

S: We still have people who accumulate gold . . . we have business men, they have got money.

B: You feel it is really there. It will never corrode, it will never vanish and you can count on it.

S: So it is something that I can count on.

K: Count on, hold on to, cling to, be attached to.

S: The me.

K: Exactly.

S: I know that I am a doctor. I can depend on that.

K: Experience. And on the other hand, tradition.

S: Tradition. I know that if I do this with a patient I will get a certain result—I may not get any good results but I'll get this result.

K: So I think that is fairly clear.

B: Yes, it is clear enough that this is part of our society.

K: Part of our conditioning.

B: Conditioning, that we want something secure and permanent. At least we think so.

S: I think there is a feeling in the West of wanting immortality.

K: That's the same thing.

B: Wouldn't you say that in so far as thought can project time, that it wants to be able to project everything as far as possible into the future? In other words the anticipation of what is coming is already the present feeling. If you anticipate that something bad may come you already feel bad.

K: That's right.

B: Therefore you would want to get rid of that.

S: So you anticipate that it won't happen.

B: That it will all be good.

S: Right.

B: I would say that security would be the anticipation that everything will be good in the future . . .

K: Good.

S: It will continue.

B: It will become better; if it is not so good now it will certainly become better.

S: So then security is becoming?

K: Yes, becoming, perfecting, becoming.

S: I see patients all the time. Their projected belief is, I will become—I will find somebody to love me; I see patients who say, "I will become the chief of the department", "I will become the most famous doctor", "I will become the best tennis player". The best.

K: Of course, of course.

B: Well, it seems it is all focused on anticipating that life is going to be good, when you say that.

K: Yes, life is going to be good.

B: But it seems to me you wouldn't raise the question unless you had a lot of experience that life is not so good. In other words it is a reaction to having had so much experience of disappointment, of suffering . . .

K: Would you say that we are not conscious of the whole movement of thought?

B: It is only natural to feel I have had a lot of experience of suffering and disappointment and danger, and now I would like to be able to anticipate that everything is going to be good. At first sight it would seem that that is quite natural. But now you are saying it is not.

K: We are saying there is no such thing as psychological security. We have defined what we mean by security. We don't have to beat it over and over.

S: No, I think we have got that.

B: Yes, but is it clear now that these hopes are really vain hopes. That should be obvious, should it?

K: Sir, there is death at the end of everything.

B: Yes.

K: You want to be secure for the next ten years, that is all, or 50 years. Afterwards it doesn't matter. Or if it does matter you believe in something—that there is god, that you will sit on his right hand or whatever it is you believe. So I am trying to find out, not only that there is no permanency psychologically, but that there is no tomorrow psychologically.

B: That hasn't yet come out.

K: Of course, of course.

B: We can say empirically that we know these hopes for security are false because first of all you say there is death, secondly you can't count on anything; materially everything changes.

K: Everything is in flux.

B: Mentally everything in your head is changing all the time. You can't count on your own feelings, you can't count on enjoying a certain thing that you enjoy now, you can't count on being healthy, you can't count on money.

K: You can't rely on your wife, you can't rely—on anything.

S: Right.

B: So that is a fact. But I am saying that you are suggesting something deeper.

K: Yes, sir.

B: But we don't base ourselves only on that observation.

K: No, that is very superficial.

S: Yes, I am with you there.

K: So, if there is no real security, basic, deep, then is there a tomorrow, psychologically? Then you take away all hope. If there is no tomorrow you take away all hope.

B: What you mean by tomorrow is the tomorrow in which things will get better?

K: Better, more—greater success, greater understanding, greater . . .

B: . . . more love.

K: . . . more love, always that.

S: I think that is a little quick. I think that there is a jump there because as I hear you, I hear you saying there is no security.

K: But it is so.

S: But for me to say—to really say, "I know there is no security" . . .

K: Why don't you say that?

S: That is what I am getting at. Why don't I say that?

B: Well isn't it a fact—just an observed fact that there isn't anything you can count on psychologically?

S: Right. But you see I think there is an action there. Krishnaji is asking, "Why don't you say there is no security?" Why don't I?

K: Do you, when you hear there is no security, see it as an abstracted idea or as an actual fact? Like that table, like your hand there, or those flowers?

S: I think it mostly becomes an idea.

K: That is just it.

B: Why should it become an idea?

S: That, I think, is the question. Why does it become an idea?

K: Is it part of your training?

S: Part—yes. Part of my conditioning.

K: Part of a real objection to seeing things as they are.

S: That's right.

B: If you try to see that there is no security, something seems to be there which is trying to protect itself—let us say that it seems to be a fact that the self is there. Do you see what I am driving at?

K: Of course.

B: And if the self is there it requires security, and this creates a resistance to accepting as a fact that there is no security, and puts it as an idea only. It seems that the factuality of the self being there has not been denied. The apparent factuality.

K: Is it that you refuse to see things as they are? Is it that one refuses to see that one is stupid?—not you—I mean one is stupid. To acknowledge that one is stupid is already . . .

S: Yes. You say to me, "You refuse to acknowledge that you are stupid"—let us say it is me—that means then that I have got to do something . . .

K: No. Not yet. Action comes through perception, not through ideation.

S: I am glad you are getting into this.

B: Doesn't it seem that as long as there is the sense of self, the self must say that it is perfect?

K: Of course, of course.

S: Now what makes it so hard for me to destroy this need for security? Why can't I do it?

K: No, no. It is not how you can do it. You see you are already entering into the realm of action.

S: That I think is the crucial point.

K: I say first see it. And from that perception action is inevitable.

S: All right. Now to see insecurity. Do you see insecurity? Do you actually see it?

K: No. No. No. Do you actually see that you are clinging to something, some belief which gives you security?

S: OK.

K: I cling to this house. I am safe. It gives me a sense of pride, a sense of possession; it gives me a sense of physical and therefore psychological security.

S: Right, and a place to go.

K: A place to go. But I may walk out and be killed and I have lost everything. There might be an earthquake and everything gone. Do you actually *see* it? The seeing, the perception, of that is total action with regard to security.

S: I can see that that is the total action.

K: No, that is an idea, still.

S: Yes, you're right. I begin to see that this whole structure is the way I see everything in the world—right? I begin to see her, the wife, I begin to see these people—they fit into that structure.

K: You see them, and your wife, through the image you have about them.

S: Right. And through the function they are serving.

B: Their relation to you, yes.

K: Yes.

S: That is right. That's the function they serve.

K: The picture, the image, the conclusion is the security.

S: That's right.

B: Yes, but why does it present itself as so real? I see that there is a thought, a process which is driving on, continually . . .

K: Are you asking why has this image, this conclusion, become so fantastically real?

B: Yes. It seems to be standing there real, and everything is referred to it.

K: More real than the marbles, than the hills.

B: Than anything, yes.

S: More real than anything.

K: Why?

S: It is hard to say why. Because it would give me security.

K: No. We are much further than that.

B: Because, suppose abstractly and ideally you can see the whole thing as no security at all. I mean just looking at it professionally and abstractly.

S: That is putting the cart before the horse.

B: No, I am just saying that if it were some simple matter, with that much proof you would have already accepted it.

S: Right.

B: But when it comes to this, no proof seems to work.

S: Right. Nothing seems to work.

B: You say all that, but here I am presented with the solid reality of myself and my security and there is a sort of reaction which seems to say, well that may be possible but it is really only words. The real thing is me.

S: But there is more than that. Why has it such potency? I mean, it seems to take on such importance.

35

B: Well, maybe. But I am saying that the real thing is me, which is all important.

S: There is no question about it. Me, me—me is important.

K: Which is an idea.

B: We can see abstractly that it is just an idea. The question is how do you break into this process?

K: I think we can break into it, or break through it, or get beyond it only through perception.

B: The trouble is that all that we have been talking about is in the form of ideas. They may be correct ideas but they won't break into this.

S: Right.

B: Because this dominates the whole of thought.

S: That is right. I mean you could even ask why are we here. We are here because we want to . . .

K: No, sir. Look: If I feel my security lies in some image I have, a picture, a symbol, a conclusion or an ideal, I would put it not as an abstraction but bring it down. You see it is so. I believe in something. Actually. Now I say, why do I believe?

B: Well have you actually done that?

K: No, I haven't because I have no beliefs. I have no picture, I don't go in for all those kinds of games. I said "if".

S: If, right.

K: Then I would bring the abstracted thing into a perceptive reality.

S: To see my belief, is that it?

K: See it.

S: To see my belief. Right. To see that 'me' in operation.

K: Yes, if you like to put it that way. Sir, wait a minute. Take a simple thing. Have you a conclusion about something? A concept?

S: Yes.

K: Now wait a bit. How is that brought about? Take a simple thing—a concept that I am an Englishman.

B: The trouble is that we probably don't feel attached to such concepts.

K: All right.

S: Let's take one that is real for me. Take the one about me being a doctor.

K: A concept.

S: That is a concept. That is a conclusion based on training, based on experience, based on the enjoyment of the work.

K: Which means what? A doctor means—the conclusion means he is capable of certain activities.

S: Right, OK. Let's take it. Concretely.

K: Work at it.

S: So now I have got this concrete fact that I have had this training, that I get this pleasure from the work, I get a kind of feedback . . .

K: Yes, sir. Move.

S: All right. Now that is my belief. That belief that I am a doctor is based on all that, that concept.

K: Yes.

S: OK. Now I continually act to continue that.

K: Yes, sir, that is understood. Therefore you have a conclusion. You have a concept that you are a doctor.

S: Right.

K: Based on knowledge, experience, everyday activity.

S: Right.

K: Pleasure and all the rest of it.

S: Right.

K: So what is real in that? What is true in that? Real, meaning actual.

S: Well that is a good question. What is actual?

K: Wait. What is actual in that? Your training.

S: Right.

K: Your knowledge.

S: Right.

K: Your daily operation.

S: Right.

K: That's all. The rest is a conclusion.

B: But what is the rest?

K: The rest: I am very much better than somebody else.

B: Or else this thing is going to keep me occupied in a good way.

K: In a good way. I will never be lonely.

S: Right.

B: But isn't there also a certain fear that if I don't have this then things will be pretty bad?

K: Of course.

S: Right, OK.

B: And that fear seems to spur me on . . .

K: Of course. And if the patients don't turn up . . .

B: Then I have no money, fear.

K: Fear.

S: No activity.

K: So loneliness. So be occupied.

S: Be occupied doing this, completing this concept. OK. Do you realize how important that is to all people, to be occupied?

K: Of course, sir.

S: Do you get the meat of that?

K: Of course.

S: How important it is to people to be occupied. I can see them running around.

K: Sir, a housewife is occupied. Remove that occupation and she says: Please . . .

B: "What shall I do?"

S: We know that as a fact. Since we put electrical equipment into the houses the women are going crazy, they have nothing to do with their time.

K: The result of this is the effect on the children—don't talk to me about it.

S: Right, OK. Let's go on. Now we have got this fact.

K: Now is this occupation an abstraction? Or actuality?

S: Now this is an actuality. I am actually occupied.

K: No.

B: What is it?

K: You are actually occupied—eh?

S: Yes.

K: Daily.

S: Daily.

B: Well what do you really mean by occupied?

S: What do you mean?

B: Well, I can say I am actually engaged in all these occupations—that is clear. I mean I am seeing patients as the doctor.

S: You are doing your thing.

B: I am doing my thing, getting my reward and so on. Being occupied seems to me to have a psychological meaning. There was something I once saw on television about a woman who was highly disturbed; it showed on the electro-encephalograph, but when she was occupied doing arithmetical sums the electro-encephalograph went beautifully smooth. She stopped doing the sums and it went all over the place. Therefore she had to keep on doing something to keep the brain working right.

K: Which means what?

B: Well what does it mean?

K: A mechanical process.

S: That's right.

B: It seems the brain starts jumping all over the place unless it has this thing.

K: A constant . . .

B: Content.

K: So you have reduced yourself to a machine.

S: Don't say it! No, it's not fair. But it is true. I have, I mean I feel there is a mechanical . . .

K: . . . response.

S: Oh, yes—commitment.

K: Of course.

B: But why does the brain begin to go so wild when it is not occupied? That seems to be a common experience.

K: Because in occupation there is security.

B: There is order.

K: Order.

S: In occupation there is a kind of mechanical order.

B: Right. So we feel our security really means we want order, is that right?

K: That's it.

B: We want order inside the brain. We want to be able to project order into the future, for ever.

S: That's right. But would you say that you can get it by mechanical order?

B: Then you get dissatisfied with it; you say, "I am getting sick of this mechanical life, I want something more interesting."

K: That is where the gurus come in!

B: Then the thing goes wild again. The mechanical order won't satisfy it. It works only for a little while.

S: I don't like the way something is slipping in there. We are going right from one thing to another. I am working for satisfaction.

B: I am looking for some regular order which is good, do you see? And I think that by my job as a doctor I am getting it.

S: Yes.

B: But after a while I begin to feel it is too repetitious. I am getting bored.

S: OK. But suppose that doesn't happen? Suppose some people remain satisfied with their jobs?

B: Well they don't really. I mean then they become dull.

K: Quite. Mechanical. And you stop that mechanism and the brain goes wild.

S: That's right.

B: Right. So they may feel they are a bit dull and they would like some entertainment, or something more interesting and exciting. And therefore there is a contradiction, there is conflict and confusion.

K: Sir, Dr Shainberg is asking what is disturbing him. He feels he hasn't got his teeth into it.

S: You are right.

K: What is disturbing you?

S: Well, it is this feeling that people will say that . . .

K: No, *you* say, *you*.

S: Let's say I can get this order from occupying myself with something I like.

K: Go on. Proceed.

S: I do something I like and it gets boring, let's say, or it might get repetitious, but then I will find new parts of it. And then I'll do that some more because that gives me pleasure, you see. I mean I get a satisfaction out of it.

B: Right.

S: So I keep doing more of that.

K: You move from one mechanical process, get bored with it, and move to another mechanical process.

S: That's right.

K: Get bored with it and keep going.

S: That's right. That's it.

K: And you call that living.

S: That is what I call living.

B: I see that the trouble is that I now try to be sure that I can keep on doing this, because I can always anticipate a future when I won't be able to do it. I will be a bit too old for it, or else I'll fail. I'll lose the job or something. So I still have insecurity in that order.

K: Essentially it is mechanical disorder.

S: Masking itself as order.

K: Now, wait a minute. Do you see this? Or is it still an abstraction? Because you know, as Dr Bohm will tell you, idea means observation, the original meaning is observation. Do you observe this?

S: I see that, yes.

B: Then the point is, are you driven to this because you are

41

frightened of the instability of the brain? If you are doing something because you are trying to run away from the instability of the brain, that is already disorder.

S: Yes, yes.

B: In other words that will be merely masking disorder.

S: Yes. Well then you are suggesting that this is the natural disorder of the brain?

B: No, I am saying that the brain without occupation tends to go into disorder.

K: In a mechanical process the brain feels secure, and when that mechanical process is disturbed it becomes insecure and disordered.

S: Then gets caught up again in the mechanical process.

K: Again and again and again and again.

S: It never stays with that insecurity.

K: No. When it perceives this process it is still mechanical. And therefore there is disorder.

B: The question is why does the brain get caught in mechanism?

K: Because it is the safest, the most secure way of living.

B: Well, it appears that way, but it is actually very . . .

K: Not appears, it is so for the time being.

B: For the time being, but in the long run it is not.

S: Are you saying we are time-bound, conditioned to be time-bound?

K: No. Conditioned by our tradition, by our education, by the culture we live in, to operate mechanically.

S: We take the easy way.

K: The easy way.

B: At the beginning the brain makes a mistake, let's say, and says "This is safer"—but somehow it fails to be able to see that it has made a mistake; it holds to this mistake. In the beginning you might call it an innocent mistake; it says, "This looks safer and I will follow it" and it continues in this mechanical process rather than seeing that it is wrong.

K: You are asking: Why doesn't it see that this mechanical process is essentially disorder?

B: That it is essentially disorder and dangerous.

K: Dangerous.

B: It is totally delusory.

S: Why isn't there some sort of feedback? In other words I do something and it comes out wrong. At some point I ought to realize that. Why haven't I seen that my life is mechanical?

K: Now wait. You see it?

S: But I don't.

K: Wait. Why is it mechanical?

S: Well, it is mechanical because it is all action and reaction.

K: Why is it mechanical?

S: It is repetitious.

K: It is mechanical.

S: It is mechanical. I want it to be easy. I feel that it gives me the most security to keep it mechanical. I get a boundary. It is mechanical because it is repetitious . . .

K: You haven't answered my question.

S: I know I haven't! I am not sure what your question is.

K: Why has it become mechanical?

S: Why?

B: Why does it remain mechanical?

K: Why does it become and remain mechanical?

S: I think it remains mechanical . . . it is the thing we began with.

K: No. Pursue it. Why does it remain mechanical?

S: What has caused us to accept this mechanical way of living? I am not sure I can answer that.

K: Look. Wouldn't you be frightened?

S: I would see the uncertainty.

K: No, no. If the mechanical life one lives suddenly stopped, wouldn't you be frightened?

S: Yes.

B: Wouldn't there be some danger?

K: That, of course. There is a danger that things might . . .

S: . . . go to pieces.

K: . . . go to pieces.

S: It is deeper than that.

K: Wait. Find out. Come on.

S: It is not just that there is a genuine danger, that I would be frightened. It feels like things take on a terribly, moment-by-moment effect.

K: No, sir. Total order would give complete security, wouldn't it?

S: Yes.

K: The brain wants total order.

S: Right.

K: Otherwise it can't function properly. Therefore it accepts the mechanical, hoping it won't lead to disaster. Hoping it will find order in that.

B: Could you say that perhaps in the beginning the brain accepted this not knowing that this mechanicalism would bring disorder—that it just went into it in an innocent state?

K: Yes.

B: And now it is caught in a trap, and somehow it maintains this disorder, it doesn't want to get out of it.

K: Because it is frightened of greater disorder.

B: Yes. It says all that I've built up may go to pieces. In other words I am not in the same situation as when I first went into the trap because now I have built up a great structure. I'm afraid that structure will go to pieces.

K: Yes, but what I am trying to get at is that the brain needs this order, otherwise it can't function. It finds order in the mechanical process because it is trained from childhood—do as you are told, etc. There is a conditioning going on right from the start to live a mechanical life.

B: And at the same time the fear of giving up this mechanism.

K: Of course, of course.

B: In other words you are thinking all the time that without this mechanism everything will go to pieces, especially the brain.

K: Which means the brain must have order. And finds order in a mechanical way. Now do you see that actually the mechanical way of living leads to disorder? Which is tradition. If I live entirely in the past, which I think is very orderly, what takes place? I am already dead and I can't meet anything.

S: I am repeating myself always, right?

K: So I say, "Please don't disturb my tradition!" Every human being says, "I have found something which gives me order, a belief, a hope, this, or that, so leave me alone."

S: Right.

K: And life isn't going to leave him alone. So then he gets frightened and establishes another mechanical habit. Now do you see this whole thing? And therefore an instant action clearing it all away, and therefore order. The brain says at last I have an order, which is absolutely indestructible.

B: That doesn't follow logically.

K: It would follow logically if you go into it.

B: Go into it. Can we reach a point where it really follows necessarily?

K: I think we can only go into it if you perceive the mechanical structure which the brain has developed, attached and cultivated.

S: Can I share with you something I see as you are talking? I see it like this. Don't get impatient with me too quickly. I see it this way. Flashing through my mind are various kinds of interchange between people. The way they talk, the way I talk to them at a party. It is all about what happened before. You find them telling you who they are, in terms of their past. I can see what they will be. Like one guy who said, "I have just published my thirteenth book." It is very important to him that I get that information, see. And I see this. And I see this elaborate structure. This guy has got it into his head that I am going to think this about him, and then he is going to go to his university and they will think that about him. He is always living like that and the whole structure is elaborate—right?

K: Are you doing that?

S: When did you stop beating your wife! Of course I am doing it. I

45

am doing it right now. And seeing the structure right now in all of us.

K: But do you see that fragmentary action is mechanical action?

S: That's right. It is there, Krishnaji. That is the way we are.

K: And therefore political action can never solve any human problems. Nor can the scientist—he is another fragment.

S: But do you realize what you are saying? Let us really look at what you are saying. This is the way it is. This is the way life is.

K: That's right.

S: Right? This is the way it is. Years and years and years . . .

K: Therefore why don't you change it?

S: But this is the way it is. We live in terms of our structures. We live in terms of history. We live in terms of our mechanics. We live in terms of our form. This is the way we live.

K: It means that when the past meets the present and ends there, a totally different thing takes place.

S: Yes. But the past doesn't meet the present so often. I mean . . .

K: I mean it is taking place now.

S: Now. Right now. Right. We are saying it now.

K: Therefore can you stop there?

S: We must see it totally.

K: No. The fact. The simple fact. The past meets the present. That is a fact.

B: Let us say how does the past meet the present? Let us go into that.

S: How does the past meet the present?

B: Well, just briefly, I think that when the past meets the present the past stops acting. What it means is that thought stops acting so that order comes about.

S: Do you think the past meets the present, or the present meets the past?

K: How do you meet me?

S: I meet you in the present.

K: No. How do you meet me? With all the memories, all the

46

images, the reputation, the words, the pictures, the symbols—with all that, which is the past, you meet me now.

S: That's right. That's right. I come to you with a . . .

K: The past is meeting the present.

S: And then?

K: Ends there. Does not move forward.

S: Can it stop? What is the past meeting present? What is that action?

K: I will show it to you. I meet you with the past, my memories, but you might have changed in the meantime. So I never meet you. I meet you with the past.

S: Right. That is a fact.

K: That is a fact. Now if I don't have that movement going on . . .

S: But I do.

K: Of course you do. But I say that that is disorder. I can't meet you then.

S: Right. How do you know that?

K: I don't know it. I only know the fact that when the past meets the present and continues, it is one of the factors of time, movement, bondage, fear, and so on. If, when the past meets the present, one sees this, one is fully aware of this, completely aware of this movement, then it stops. Then I meet you as though for the first time, then there is something fresh. It is like a new flower coming out.

S: Yes.

K: I think we will go on this afternoon. We haven't really tackled the root of all this. The root, the cause, of all this disturbance, this turmoil, travail and anxiety.

B: Why should the brain be in this wild disorder?

K: I know, wild. You, Dr Shainberg, who are a doctor, an analyst, you have to ask that fundamental question—Why? Why do human beings live this way?

DIALOGUE III

May 18 – afternoon

KRISHNAMURTI: Shall we start where we left off? We were asking, weren't we, why do human beings live this way?

Dr Shainberg: What is the root?

K: The turmoil, the confusion, the sorrow behind it all, the conflict, the violence. And so many people offer different ways of solving the problems—the gurus, the priests all over the world, the thousands of books, everybody offering a new solution, a new method, a new way of solving the problems. And I am sure this has been going on for a million years. "Do this and you will be all right. Do that and you will be all right." But nothing seems to have succeeded in making man live in order, happily, intelligently, without this chaotic activity going on. Why do we human beings live this way—in this appalling misery? Why?

S: Well, I have often said they do it because the very sorrow, the very turmoil, the very problems themselves, give them a sense of security.

Dr Bohm: I don't really think so. I think people just get used to it. Whatever happens you get used to it and you come to miss it after a while just because you are used to it. But that doesn't explain why it is there.

K: I was reading the other day that in 5,000 years there have been 5,000 wars—and we are still going on.

S: That's right. A guy said to me once that he wanted to go to Vietnam to fight because otherwise his life was every night at the bar.

K: I know, but that isn't the reason. Is it that we like it?

S: It is not that we like it; it is almost that we like not liking it.

K: Have we all become neurotic?

48

S: Yes. The whole thing is neurotic.

K: Are you saying that?

S: Yes. The whole of society is neurotic.

K: Which means that entire humanity is neurotic?

S: I think so. This is the argument we have all the time: Is society sick? And then if you say society is sick, what is the value you are using for comparison?

K: Yourself, who is neurotic.

S: Right.

K: So when you are faced with this, that human beings live this way and have accepted it for millennia, you say, "Well they are all half crazy—demented, corrupt from top to bottom", and then I come along and ask why?

S: Why do we keep it up? Why are we crazy? I see it with my children. They spend 50 hours a week in front of the television box. That is their whole life. My children laugh at me, all their friends are doing it.

K: No, moving beyond that—why?

S: Why? Without it—what?

K: No: not without it, what.

S: That is what we run into.

B: No, that is very secondary. You see, as we were saying this morning, I think we get to depend on it to occupy us, and war would seem some release from the boredom of the pub, or whatever, but that is secondary.

K: And also when I go to fight a war, all responsibility is taken away from me. Somebody else becomes responsible—the general . . .

S: Right.

B: In the old days people used to think that war would be a glorious thing. When the first world war started in England everybody was in a state of high elation.

K: So looking at this panorama of horror—I feel this very strongly because I travel all over the place and I see this extraordinary phenomenon going on everywhere—I say why do people live this way, accept these things? We have become cynical.

B: Nobody believes anything can be done about it.

S: That's it.

K: Is it that we feel that we cannot do anything about it?

S: That's for sure.

B: That's been an old story. People say human nature . . .

K: . . . can never be altered.

B: Yes. That is not new at all.

K: Not new.

S: But it's certainly true that people feel—let's not say people—*we* feel, like I said this morning, that this is the way it is, this is the way we live.

K: I know, but why don't you change it? You see your son looking at the television for 50 hours; you see your son going off to war, killed, maimed, blinded—for what?

B: Many people have said that they don't accept that human nature is this way, that they will try to change it, and it hasn't worked. The Communists tried it; others tried it. There has been so much bad experience, which all adds up to the idea that human nature doesn't change.

S: You know when Freud came along, he made history: he never said psycho-analysis is to change people. He said we can only study people.

K: I am not interested in that. I know that. I don't have to read Freud, or Jung, or you, or anybody, it is there in front of me.

S: Right. So let's say we know this fact about people, they don't try to change.

K: So what is preventing them?

B: People have tried to change in many cases, but . . .

S: OK. But now let's say that they don't try to change.

K: They do. In a dozen ways they try to change.

S: Right.

K: But essentially they are the same.

B: You see, I think people cannot find out how to change human nature.

K: Is that it?

B: Well, whatever methods have been tried are entirely . . .

S: Is that it? Or is it the fact that the very nature of the way they want to change is part of the process itself?

B: No.

K: That's what he is saying.

B: No, but I am saying both. I say the first part is that whatever people have tried has not been guided by a correct understanding of human nature.

S: So it is guided by this very process itself? Right? By the incorrectness?

B: Yes, let's take the Marxists who say that human nature can be improved, but only when the whole economical and political structure has been altered.

K: They have tried to alter it but human nature . . .

B: . . . they can't alter it, you see, because human nature is such that they can't really alter it.

S: They make a mechanical change.

K: Look at it, sir: take yourself—sorry to be personal—but if you don't mind, you be the victim.

S: Pig in the middle.

.K: Right. Why don't you change?

S: Well, the immediate feel of it is that there is still . . . I guess I shall have to say there is some sort of false security—the fragmentation, the immediate pleasures that are got from the fragmentation. In other words there is still that movement of fragmentation. That's how come there is not the change. It is not seeing the whole thing.

K: Are you saying that political action, religious action, social action, are all fighting each other? And we *are* that.

S: Right.

K: Is that what you are saying?

S: Yes, I am saying that. My immediate response is: Why don't I change? What is it that keeps me from seeing the total? I don't know. I keep coming up with a kind of feeling that I am getting something from not changing.

K: Is it the entity that wishes to change—which sets the pattern of change, and therefore the pattern is always the same under a different colour? I don't know if I am making myself clear?

S: Could you say it another way?

K: I want to change, and I plan what to change, how to bring about this change.

S: Right.

K: The planner is always the same.

S: That's right.

K: But the patterns change.

S: That's right. Yes. I have an image of what I want.

K: So the patterns change, but I, who want to change, create the patterns of change.

S: That's right.

K: So I am the old and the patterns are the new but the old is always conquering the new.

S: Right.

B: But when I do that I don't feel that I am the old . . .

K: . . . of course.

B: I really don't feel I am involved in that old stuff I want to change.

K: It has been said a hundred million times. Do this and you will be transformed. You try to do it but the centre is always the same.

B: And each person who does it feels that it has never happened before.

K: Never before. Yes. My experience through reading some book is entirely different, but the experiencer is the same . . .

B: The same old thing, right.

K: I think that is one of the root causes of it.

S: Yes, yes.

B: It is a kind of sleight-of-hand trick whereby the thing which is causing the trouble is put into the position of the thing that is trying to make the change. It is a deception.

K: I am deceiving myself all the time by saying I am going to change that, become that. You read some book and say, "Yes how true that is, I am going to live according to that." But the me who is going to live according to that is the same old me.

S: Right, yes. That's right. We run into this with patients. For instance, the patient will say, the doctor is going to be the one who is going to help me. But when I see that that doctor is . . .

K: . . . is like me.

S: . . . is like me, he is not going to be able to help. Then the patient goes to someone else—most of them go to another therapy.

K: Another guru. After all they are all men too. A new guru, or an old guru—it is all the same old stuff.

S: You are really getting at the issue, that the root is this belief that something, someone, can help you.

K: No, the root remains the same—and we trim the branches.

B: I think the root is something we don't see because we put it in the position of the one who is supposed to be seeing.

K: Yes.

S: Say that another way.

B: It is a sort of a conjuring trick. We don't see the root because the root is put into the position of somebody who is looking for the root. I don't know if you see it.

K: Yes. The root says I am looking for the root.

S: Right.

B: It is like the man who says he is looking for his glasses, and he has got them on.

S: Or like that Sufi story—you know the story?—a guy is looking for a key he has lost. The Sufi comes along and sees the guy crawling around under the lamp-post, and he says, "What are you doing?" "I am looking for my key." "Did you lose it here?" "No, I lost it over there but there's more light over here."

B: We throw the light on the other part.

K: Yes, sir. So if I want to change I don't follow anybody because they are all like the rest of the gang. I don't accept any authority in all this. Authority arises only when I am confused. When I am in disorder.

S: That's right.

K: So I say, can I completely change at the very root?

B: Let's look at that: there seems confusion in the language because you say "I".

K: Confusion in the language, I know.

B: You say I am going to change and it is not clear what you mean by I.

K: The I is the root.

B: The I is the root, so how can I change?

K: That is the whole point.

B: You see the language is confusing because you say I have got to change at the root, but I am the root. So what is going to happen?

S: What is going to happen, yes?

K: No, no. How am I not to be I?

B: Well, what do you mean by that?

S: How am I not to be I? Let's roll it back a second. You state you are not going to accept any authority.

K: Who is my authority? Who? They have all told me, "Do this, do that, do the other. Read this book and you will change. Follow this system, you will change. Identify yourself with god, you will change." But I remain exactly as I was before—in sorrow, in misery, in confusion, looking for help, and I choose the help which suits me most. Umpteen different ways have been tried to change man. Rewarding him, punishing him, promising him. Nothing has brought about this miraculous change. And it is a miraculous change.

S: It would be, yes, yes.

K: It is so. So, seeing this, I reject all authority. It is a reasonable, sane rejection. Now how do I proceed? I have got 50 years to live. What is the correct action?

S: What is the correct action to live properly?

K: If everybody said, "I can't help you, you have to do it yourself, look at yourself", then the whole thing would begin to act. Here is a man who says, "I am neurotic and I won't go to any other kind of neurotic to make me sane". What does he do? He doesn't accept authority, because he has created the authority out of his disorder.

B: Well, that is merely the hope that somebody knows what to do.

K: Yes.

B: Because I feel this chaos is too much for me and I just assume that somebody else can tell me what to do. But that comes out of this confusion.

S: Yes, the disorder creates the authority.

K: In the school here I have been saying: If you behave properly there is no authority. The behaviour we have all agreed to—punctuality, cleanliness, this or that: if you really see it you have no authority.

S: Yes, I see that. That I think is a key point. That the disorder itself creates the need for authority.

B: It doesn't actually create a need for it. It creates among people the impression that they need authority to correct the disorder. That would be more exact.

K: So let's start from there. In the rejection of authority I am beginning to become sane. I say that now I know I am neurotic what shall I do? What is correct action in my life? Can I ever find it—being neurotic?

S: Right.

K: I can't. So I won't ask what is the right action—I will now say: Can I free my mind from being neurotic? Is it possible? I won't go to Jerusalem, I won't go to Rome, I won't go to any doctors. Because I am very serious now. I am deadly serious because this is my life.

B: You have to be so serious because of the immense pressure to escape . . .

K: I won't.

B: . . . you won't, but I am saying that one will feel at this juncture that there will probably be an intense pressure towards escape, saying this is too much.

K: No. No, sir. You see what happens . . .

S: What happens?

K: . . . when I reject authority I have much more energy.

B: Yes, if you reject authority.

K: Because I am now concentrated to find out for myself. I am not looking to anybody.

S: That's right. In other words, I then have to be really open to "what is", that is all I have got.

K: So what shall I do?

S: When I am really open to "what is"?

K: Not open. Here I am, here is a human being, caught in all this, what shall he do?—rejecting all authority, knowing that social discipline is immoral . . .

S: Then there is intense alertness . . .

K: No. Tell me. Tell me—you are a doctor, tell me what I am to do. I reject you.

S: Right.

K: Because you are not my doctor, you are not my authority.

S: Right.

K: You can't tell me what to do, because you are confused yourself.

S: Right.

K: So you have no right to tell me what to do. So I come to you as a friend, and say let's find out. Because you are serious and I am serious. Let's see how . . .

S: . . . we can work together.

K: No, no, be careful. I am not working together.

S: You are not going to work together?

K: No. We are investigating together. Working together means co-operation.

S: Right.

K: I am not co-operating. I say you are like me. What are we going to co-operate with?

S: In order to co-operatively investigate.

K: No. Because you are like me, confused, miserable, unhappy, neurotic.

S: Right, right.

K: So I say, how can we co-operate? We can only co-operate in neuroticism.

S: That's right. So what are we going to do?

K: So can we investigate together?

S: How can we investigate together if we are both neurotic?

K: I say look, I am going first to see in what ways I am neurotic.

S: OK. Let's look at it.

K: Yes, look at it. In what way am I neurotic—a human being, who comes from New York, or Tokyo, or Delhi, or Moscow, or wherever it is? He says, I know I am neurotic, the leaders of the world are neurotic and I am part of it—I am the world and the world is me—so I can't look to anybody. Do you see what that does?

S: It puts you straight up there in front.

K: It gives you a tremendous sense of integrity.

S: Right. You have to fall on your hands and run with it.

K: Now can I—I being a human being—can I look at my neuroticism? Is it possible to see my neuroticism? What is neuroticism? What makes me neurotic? All the things that have been put into me, which make the me. Can my consciousness empty all that?

S: Your consciousness is that thought.

K: Of course.

B: Is it only that?

K: For the moment I am limiting it to that.

B: That is my consciousness. That proliferation of my fragmentation, my thought, is my neuroticism. Isn't that right?

K: Of course. It is a tremendous question, you follow? Can I, can the consciousness of man, which began five, ten million years ago, with all the things that have been put into it, generation after generation, generation after generation, from the beginning until now—can you take the whole of it and look at it?

S: Can you take the whole of it—that's not clear. How can you take the whole of it and look at it?

B: It seems there's a language problem there: You say you *are* that, how can you look at it?

K: I'll show you in a minute. We'll go into it.

B: I mean there is a difficulty in stating it.

57

K: I know, stating it. The words are wrong.

B: Yes, the words are wrong. So we shouldn't take these words too literally.

K: Not too literally, of course.

B: Could we say that the words can be used flexibly?

K: No, the word is not the thing.

B: But we are using words and the question is how are we to understand them? You see they are in some way an . . .

K: . . . an impediment and . . .

B: . . . in some way a clue to what we are talking about. It seems to me that one trouble with words is the way we take them. We take them to mean something very fixed.

K: Now, can you look at it without the word? Is that possible? The word is not the thing. The word is a thought. And as a human being I realize I am neurotic—neurotic in the sense that I believe, I live in conclusions, in memories, which are neurotic processes.

S: In words.

K: In words. Words, pictures and reality. I believe in something. My belief is very real; it may be illusory—all beliefs are illusory but because I believe so strongly they are real to me.

B: Right.

K: So can I look at the nature of the belief, how it arose—look at it? Can you look at that fact that you have a belief? Whatever it is, god, the State, or whatever.

S: But I believe it is true.

K: No, no. Can you look at that belief?

S: There is a belief and not a fact.

K: Ah, no. It is a reality to you when you believe in it.

S: Right, but how am I going to look at it if I really believe it? I say there is a god. Now you are telling me to look at my belief in the god.

K: Why do you believe? Who asked you to believe? What is the necessity of god? Not that I am an atheist, but I am asking you.

S: God is there for me, if I believe.

K: Then there is no investigation, it has stopped, you have blocked yourself; you have shut the door.

58

S: That's right. But you see we have got such beliefs. How can we get at this? Because I think we have loads of these unconscious beliefs that we don't really shake. Like the belief in the me.

B: I think a deeper question is how the mind sets up reality. I mean, if I look at things I may think they are real. That may be an illusion but when it comes it seems real. Even with objects, you can say a word and it becomes real when you describe it that way. And therefore in some way the word sets up in the brain a construction of reality. Then everything is referred to that construction of reality.

S: How are we to investigate that?

K: What created that reality? Would you say that everything thought has created is a reality—except nature?

B: Thought didn't create nature.

K: No, of course not.

B: Can't we put it that thought can describe nature.

K: Yes, thought can describe nature—in poetry . . .

B: And also in imagination.

K: Imagination. Can we say that whatever thought has put together is reality? The chair, the table, all these electric lights, nature—thought hasn't created nature but it can describe it.

B: And also make theories about it.

K: Make theories, yes. And also the illusion thought has created is the reality.

S: Right.

B: But doesn't this construction of reality have its place, because . . .

K: Of course, of course.

B: . . . this table is real although the brain has constructed it. But at some stage we construct realities that are not there. We can see this sometimes in the shadows on a dark night constructing realities that are not there.

K: That there is a man there.

B: Yes. And also tricks and illusions are possible by conjurers. But then it goes further and we say that mentally we construct a logical reality, which seems intensely real, very strong. But it seems to me the question is: What is it that thought does to give that sense of reality, to construct reality? Can we watch that?

K: What does thought do to bring about, to create, that reality?

S: You mean like if you talk to someone who believes in God, he says to you that is real. And if you talk to somebody who really believes in the self. I talk to many people, to many psychotherapists—they say the self is real, that it exists, it is a thing. You heard a psychotherapist once say to Krishnaji, "We know the ego exists."

B: Well, it is not only that. I think what happens is that the illusion builds up very fast once you construct the reality. It builds up a tremendous structure, a cloud of support around it.

K: So let's come to it. What are we doing now?

S: We are moving.

K: We are trying to find out what is the correct action in life. I can only find that out if there is order in me—right? Me is the disorder.

S: Right. That's right.

K: However real that me is, that is the source of disorder.

S: Right.

K: Because that separates, that divides—me and you, we and they, my nation, my god—me.

S: Right.

K: Me with its consciousness.

S: Right.

K: Can that consciousness be aware of itself? Aware, like thought thinking.

B: Thinking about itself?

K: Put it very simply: can thought be aware of its own movement?

B: Yes.

S: That's the question.

B: That's the question. It could be thought understanding its own structure.

S: And its own movement. But is it thought that is aware of itself? Or is it something else?

K: Try it. Try it. Do it now.

S: Right.

K: Do it now. Can your thought be aware of itself? Of its movement?

B: It stops.

K: What does that mean?

S: It means what it says: it stops. The observation of thought, stops thought.

K: No, don't put it that way.

S: How would you put it?

K: It is undergoing a radical change.

B: So the word "thought" is not a fixed thing.

K: No.

B: The word "thought" does not mean a fixed thing. It can change—eh?

K: That's right.

B: In perception.

K: You have told me, and other scientists have told me, that in the observation of an object through a microscope, the object undergoes a change.

B: In the quantum theory the object cannot be fixed apart from the fact of observation.

S: This is true with patients during psycho-analysis. They change automatically.

K: Forget the patient, you are the patient!

S: I am the patient, right.

K: What takes place when thought is aware of itself? You know, sir, this is an extraordinarily important thing.

B: Yes.

K: That is, can the doer be aware of his doing? I can move this vase from here to there and be aware of that moving. That is very simple. I stretch out my arm . . . But can thought be aware of itself, its movement, its activity, its structure, its nature, what it has created, what it has done in the world?

S: I want to save that question for tomorrow.

DIALOGUE IV

May 19—morning

KRISHNAMURTI: I don't think that yesterday we answered the question: Why do human beings live the way they are living? I don't think we went into it sufficiently deeply. Did we answer it?

Dr Shainberg: We got the point—but we never answered that question.

K: I was thinking about it this morning and it struck me that we hadn't answered it fully. We went into the question: Can thought observe itself?

S: Right.

Dr Bohm: Right. Yes.

K: But I think we ought to answer that other question.

B: But I think that what we said was on the way to answering it. I mean it was relevant to the answer.

K: Yes, relevant. But it is not complete.

S: No, it's not complete, it doesn't really get hold of that issue: Why do people live the way they do, and why don't they change?

K: Yes. Could we go into that a little bit before we go on?

S: Well, you know my immediate answer to that question was that they like it. We came up against that and then pulled away.

K: I think it is much deeper than that, don't you? Because if one actually transformed one's conditioning, the way one lives, one might find oneself economically in a very difficult position.

S: Right.

K: It would be going against the current, completely against the current.

B: Are you saying that it might lead to a certain objective insecurity?

K: Objective insecurity.

B: It is not merely a matter of the imagination.

K: No, no, actual insecurity.

B: Yes, because a lot of the things we are discussing are to do with some illusion of security or insecurity. In addition there is some genuine . . .

K: . . . genuine insecurity. And also doesn't it imply that you have to stand alone?

S: Definitely you would be in a totally different position.

K: Because it is being completely out of the stream. And that means you have to be alone, psychologically alone. And we ask whether human beings can stand that.

S: Well, certainly this other is to be completely together.

K: It is the herd instinct. Be together, with people, don't be alone.

S: Be like them, be with them—it is all based on competition in some way. I am better than you . . .

K: Of course, of course. It is all that.

B: Well, it is unclear because in some sense we should be together, but society, it seems to me, is giving us some false sense of togetherness which is really fragmentation.

K: Quite right. So would you say that one of the main reasons why human beings don't want to transform themselves radically, is that they are frightened of not belonging to a group, to a herd, to something definite—of standing completely alone? I think you can only co-operate from that aloneness, not the other way round.

S: People don't like to be different, that we know.

K: I once talked to an FBI man—he came to see me and he said, "Why is it that you walk alone all the time? Why are you so much alone? I see you among the hills walking alone. Why?" He thought it was very disturbing.

B: Well, I think anthropologists find that in primitive peoples the sense of belonging to the tribe is even stronger; their entire psychological structure depends on being in a tribe.

K: You would rather cling to the misery you already know than come into another kind of misery you don't know.

S: That's right. Being with others . . .

K: . . . you are safe.

B: You will be taken care of, as your mother may have taken care of you; you are gently supported. You feel that fundamentally everything will be all right because the group is large, it is wise, it knows what to do. I think there is a feeling like that, rather deep. The Church may give that feeling.

K: Yes. You have seen those animal pictures? They are always in herds.

B: Aren't people seeking from the group a sense that they have some support from the whole?

K: Of course.

B: Now isn't it possible that you are discussing an aloneness in which you have a certain security? People are seeking in the group a kind of security; well, it seems to me, that that can arise actually in aloneness.

K: Yes, that is right. In aloneness you can be completely secure.

B: I wonder if we could discuss that because it seems there is an illusion there: people feel they should have a sense of security.

K: Quite right.

B: And they are looking for it in a group, the group being representative of something universal.

K: The group is not the universal.

B: It isn't, but it is the way we think of it.

K: Of course.

B: The little child thinks the tribe is the whole world.

K: A human being, if he transforms himself, becomes alone, but that aloneness is not isolation—it is a form of supreme intelligence.

B: Yes, but could you go into that a little further about it not being isolation, because at first when you say alone—the feeling that I am entirely apart . . .

K: It is not apart.

S: All people seem to gravitate together; they have to be like other people. What would change that? Why should anybody change from that? What would such people experience when they are alone? They experience isolation.

K: I thought we had already dealt with that fairly thoroughly. When one realizes the appalling state of the world, and of oneself, the disorder, the confusion and the misery, and when one says there must be a total change, a total transformation, one has already begun to move away from all that.

S: Right. But here one is, being together . . .

K: Being together, what does it really mean?

S: I mean being in this group . . .

K: Yes, what does it really mean? Identifying oneself with the group, remaining with the group—what does it mean? What is involved in it? The group is me. I am the group.

S: Right.

K: Therefore it is like co-operating with myself.

B: Perhaps you could say as Descartes said, "I think, therefore I am"—meaning that I think implies that I am there. One says, "I am in the group, therefore I am". You see, if I am not in a group where am I? In other words I have no being at all. That is really the condition of the primitive tribe, for most of the members anyway. And there is something deep there because I feel that my very existence, my being, psychologically, is implied in being in the group. The group has made me, everything about me has come from the group. I am nothing without the group.

K: Yes, quite right. I *am* the group in fact.

B: And therefore if I am out of the group I feel everything is collapsing. I don't know where I am. I have no orientation, to life or to anything.

S: Right.

B: And therefore, you see, that might be the greatest punishment the group could inflict, to banish me.

K: Yes, look what is happening in Russia: when there is a dissenter he is banished.

B: Such banishment sort of robs him of his being. It is almost like killing him.

K: Quite. I think that is what it is, the fear of being alone. Alone is translated as being isolated from all this.

B: Could we say from the universal?

K: Yes, from the universal.

B: It seems to me you are implying that if you are really alone, genuinely alone, then you are not isolated from the universe.

K: Absolutely. On the contrary.

B: Therefore we first have to be free of this false universal.

S: This false identification with the group.

B: Identification with the group as the universal. Treating the group as if it were the universal support of my being.

S: Right, right. Now there is something more to that. What is being said is that when that localized identification with the group, that false security, is dropped, one is opened up to the participation in . . .

K: No, there is no question of participation—you are the universe.

S: You are that.

B: As a child I felt that the town I was in was the whole universe; then I found another town further away which felt almost beyond the universe, which must be the ultimate limits of all reality. So the idea of going beyond that would not have occurred to me. And I think that is how the group is treated. We know abstractly that it is not so, but the feeling you have is like that of a little child.

K: Is it then that human beings love, or hold on to, their own misery and confusion because they don't know anything else?

B: Yes.

K: The known is so far, then the unknown.

S: Right. Yes.

K: Now to be alone implies, doesn't it, to step out of the stream?

S: Of the known.

K: Step out of the stream of this utter confusion, disorder, sorrow, despair, hope and travail—to step out of all that.

S: Right.

K: And if you want to go much deeper into this, to be alone implies, doesn't it, not to carry the burden of tradition with you at all?

B: Tradition being the group, then.

K: The group. Tradition also being knowledge.

B: Knowledge, but it comes basically from the group. Knowledge is basically collective. It is collected by everybody.

K: So to be alone implies total freedom. And when there is that great freedom it is the universe.

B: Could we go into that further because to a person who hasn't seen this, it doesn't look obvious?

S: I think David is right there. To a person, to most people, I think—and I have tested this out recently—the idea, or even the deep feeling, that you are the universe, seems to be so . . .

K: Ah, sir, that is a most dangerous thing to say. How can you say you are the universe when you are in total confusion? When you are unhappy, miserable, anxious, jealous, envious how can you say you are the universe? Universe implies total order.

B: Yes, the cosmos in Greek meant order.

K: Order, of course.

B: And chaos was the opposite.

K: Yes.

S: But I . . .

K: No, listen. Universe, cosmos, means order.

S: Right.

K: And chaos is what we live with.

S: That's right.

K: How can I think I have universal order in me? That is the good old trick of the mind which says disorder is there, but inside you there is perfect order. That is an illusion. It is a concept which thought has put there and it gives me a certain hope, but it is an illusion, it has no reality. What has actual reality is the confusion.

S: Right.

K: My chaos. And I can imagine, I can project a cosmos but that is equally illusory. So I must start with the fact of what I am, which is that I am in chaos.

S: I belong to a group.

K: Chaos, chaos is the group. So to move away from that into cosmos, which is total order, means that I am alone. There is a total order which is not associated with disorder, chaos. That is alone.

B: Yes, can we go into that? Suppose several people are in that state, moving into cosmos, into order out of the chaos of society— are they all alone?

K: No, they don't feel alone there. There is only order.

B: Are they different people?

K: Sir, would you say—suppose—no I can't suppose—we three are in cosmos, there is only cosmos, not you, Dr Bohm, Dr Shainberg and me.

B: Therefore we are still alone.

K: That is, order is alone.

B: I looked up the word "alone" in the dictionary; basically it is all one.

K: All one. Yes.

B: In other words there is no fragmentation.

K: Therefore there is no three—we three. And that is marvellous, sir.

S: But you jumped away there. We have got chaos and confusion. That is what we have got.

K: So as we said, to move away from that, which is to have total order, most people are afraid. Alone, as he pointed out, is all one. Therefore there is no fragmentation, then there is cosmos.

S: Right. But most people are in confusion and chaos. That is all they know.

K: So how do you move away from that? That is the whole question.

S: That is the question. Here we are in chaos and confusion, we are not over there.

K: No, because you may be frightened of that. Frightened of an idea of being alone.

S: How can you be frightened of an idea?

B: That is easy.

K: Aren't you frightened of tomorrow? Which is an idea.

S: OK. That is an idea.

K: So they are frightened of an idea which they have projected, which says, "My God, I am alone", which means I have nobody to rely on.

S: Right, but that is an idea.

B: Well, let's go slowly. We have said that to a certain extent it is genuinely so. You are not being supported by society. You do have a certain genuine danger because you have withdrawn from the hub of society.

S: I think we are confused here. I really do because I think if we have got confusion, if we have got chaos . . .

K: Not if—it is so.

S: It is so, OK I go with you. We have got chaos and confusion, that is what we have got. Now if you have an idea about being alone while in chaos and confusion, that is just another idea, another thought, another part of the chaos. Is that right?

K: That's right.

S: OK. Now that is all we have got, chaos and confusion.

K: And in moving away from that we have the feeling we will be alone.

B: In the sense of isolated.

K: Isolated.

S: Right. That's what I am getting at.

K: We will be lonely.

S: That's right.

K: Of that we are frightened.

S: Not frightened, in terror.

K: Yes. Therefore we say, "I would rather stay where I am in my little pond than face isolation." And that may be one of the reasons why human beings don't radically change.

S: That's right.

B: That's like this primitive tribe—the worst punishment is to be banished.

S: You don't have to go to a primitive tribe. I see people and talk to people all the time; patients come to me and say, "Look, Saturday came, I couldn't stand being alone, I called up 50 people looking for somebody to be with."

B: Yes, that is much the same.

K: So that may be one of the reasons why human beings don't change.

S: Right.

K: The other is that we are so heavily conditioned to accept things as they are. We don't say to ourselves, "Why should I live this way?"

S: That is certainly true. We don't.

B: We have to get away from this conviction, that the way things are is all that can be.

K: Yes, that's right. You see, the religions have pointed this out by saying there is another world, aspire to that. This is a transient world, it doesn't matter, live as best as you can in your sorrow, and then you will be perfectly happy in the next world.

S: Right.

K: And the Communists say there is no next-world, so make the best of this world.

B: I think they would say that there is happiness in the future in this world.

K: Yes, yes. Sacrifice your children for the future, which is exactly the same thing.

B: But it seems it is a sort of transformation of the same thing: we say we want to give up this society as it is, but we invent something similar.

K: Yes, quite.

S: It has to be similar if we are inventing it.

B: Yes, but it seems it is an important point, that there is a subtle way of not being alone.

K: Quite right.

S: You mean we go ahead and make it out of the old ideas?

B: Yes. To make heaven for the future.

K: So what will make human beings change? Radically.

S: I don't know. Even the idea you are suggesting here is that it can't be different, or that it is all the same: that is part of the system itself.

K: Agreed. Now wait a minute. May I ask you a question? Why don't you change? What is preventing you?

S: I would say that it is—oh, it's a tough question. I suppose the answer would be that—I don't have any answer.

K: Because you have never asked yourself that question. Right?

S: Not radically.

K: We are asking basic questions.

S: Right. I don't really know the answer to the question.

K: Now, sir, move away from that, sir. Is it that our structure, our whole society, all religions, all culture is based on thought, and thought says, "I can't do this. Therefore an outside agency is necessary to change me."

S: Right.

K: Whether the outside agency is the environment, the leader, or God. God is your own projection of yourself, obviously. And you believe in God, you believe in some leader; you believe, but you are still the same.

S: That's right.

K: You may identify with the State and so on, but the good old me is still operating. So is it that thought doesn't see its own limit? Doesn't know, realize, that it cannot change itself?

B: Well, I think thought loses track of something; it doesn't see that it itself is behind all this.

K: Of course. We said that. Thought has produced all this chaos.

B: But thought doesn't really see this exactly.

S: What thought does in fact is to communicate through gradual change.

K: That is all the invention of thought.

S: Yes, but that is where I think the hook is.

K: No, sir, please, sir, just listen.

S: Sure.

K: Thought has put this world together. Technologically as well as psychologically. The technological world is all right, leave it alone, we won't even discuss that. It would be too absurd. But psychologically, thought has built all this world in me and outside me. And does thought realize that it has made this mess, this chaos?

B: I would say that it doesn't. It tends to look on this chaos as independently existent.

K: But it is its baby!

B: It is, but it is very hard for thought to see that. That is really what we were discussing yesterday.

K: Yes, we are coming back to that.

B: To this question of how thought gives a sense of reality. We were saying that technology deals with something that thought made, but it is actually an independent reality once it is made.

K: Like the table, like those cameras.

B: But you could say that thought also creates a reality which it calls independent, but isn't.

K: Yes, yes. So, does thought realize, is it aware, that it has created this chaos?

S: No.

K: Why not? But you, sir. Do you realize it?

S: I realize that . . .

K: Not you—does thought—you see! I have asked you a different question: Does thought, which is you, your thinking—does your thinking realize the chaos it has created?

B: Thought tends to attribute that chaos to something else, either to something outside, or to me who is inside.

K: Thought has created me.

B: But also thought has said that me is not thought, although in reality it is. Thought is treating me as a different reality.

K: Of course, of course.

B: And thought is saying that it is coming from me and therefore it doesn't take credit for what it does.

K: To me thought has created the me.

S: That's right.

K: And so "me" is not separate from thought. It is the structure of thought, the nature of thought that has made me.

S: Right.

K: Now: Does your thinking, or does your thought realize this?

S: In flashes it does.

K: No, not in flashes. You don't see that table in flashes; it is always there. We asked a question yesterday, and we stopped there: Does thought see itself in movement?

S: Right.

K: The movement has created the me, created the chaos, created the division, created the conflict, jealousy, anxiety, fear . . .

S: Right. Now what I am asking is another question. Yesterday we came to a moment where we said thought stops.

K: No. That is much later. Please just stick to one thing.

S: OK. What I am trying to get at is what is the actuality of thought seeing itself?

K: You want me to describe it?

S: No, no, I don't want you to describe it—what I am trying to get at is what is the actuality that thought sees? We get into the problem of language here—but it seems that thought sees and forgets.

K: No, no, please. I am asking a very simple question. Don't complicate it. Does thought see the chaos it has created? That's all. Which means: Is thought aware of itself as a movement? Not I am aware of thought as a movement—the I has been created by thought.

S: Right.

B: I think a question that is relevant is: Why does thought keep on going? How does it sustain itself? Because as long as it sustains itself it produces something like an independent reality, an illusion of reality.

S: What is my relationship to thought?

K: You are thought. There is no you related to thought.

S: Right. But look, look. The question is: I say to you, "What is my relationship to thought?"—and you say to me "You are thought". In some way what you say is clear, but that is still the way thought is moving for me, to say it is my relationship to thought.

B: Well, that's the point. Can this very thought stop right now?

K: Yes.

B: What is sustaining this whole thing?—at this very moment?—was the question I was trying to get at.

S: Yes, that's the question.

B: In other words, say we have a certain insight but nevertheless something happens to sustain the old process right now.

K: That's right.

S: Right now thought keeps moving.

K: No, Dr Bohm asked a very good question which we haven't answered. He said, Why does thought move?

B: When it is irrelevant to move.

K: Why is it always moving? What is movement? Movement is time—right?

S: That's too quick. Movement is time.

K: Obviously, of course. Physically, from here to London, from here to New York. And also psychologically from here to there.

S: Right.

K: I am this, I must be that.

S: Right. But if a thought is not necessarily all that . . .

K: Thought is the new movement. We are examining movement, which is thought. Look: if thought stopped there is no movement.

S: Yes, I know. I am trying—this has to be made very clear.

B: I think there is a step that might help: to ask myself what it is that makes me go on thinking or talking. I can often watch people and see they are in a hole just because they keep on talking. If they would stop talking the whole problem would vanish. I mean it is just this flow of words that comes out as if it were reality, and then they say that is my problem, it is real and I have got to think some more. There is a kind of a feedback saying, "I have got a problem, I am suffering."

S: You have got an 'I' thought.

B: Yes, I think that; therefore I have a sense that I am real. I am thinking of my suffering, and in that it is implicit that it is I who am there, that the suffering is real because I am real.

S: Right.

B: And then comes the next thought, which is: Since that is real I must think some more.

S: It feeds on itself.

B: Yes. And one of the things I must think is that I am suffering. And I am compelled to keep on thinking that thought all the time. Maintaining myself in existence. Do you see what I am driving at? That there is a feedback.

K: Which means that if thought is movement, which is time, and there is no movement I am dead! I am dead.

74

B: Yes, if that movement stops, then the sense that I am there being real must go, because the sense that I am real is the result of thinking.

K: Do you see this is extraordinary?

S: Of course it is.

K: No, no, actually. In actuality, not in theory. One realizes thought is movement—right?

S: Right.

B: And in this movement it creates an image of . . .

K: . . . of me . . .

B: . . . that is supposed to be moving.

K: Yes, yes. Now, when that movement stops there is no me. The me is time, put together by time, which is thought.

S: Right.

K: So do you, listening to this, realize the truth of it? Not the verbal, logical statement, but the truth of such an amazing thing? Therefore there is an entirely different action. The action of thought as movement brings about a fragmentary action, a contradictory action. When the movement as thought comes to an end there is total action.

B: Can you say then that whatever technical thought brings about has an order?

K: Of course.

B: In other words it doesn't mean that thought is permanently gone.

K: No, no.

S: It can still be a movement in its proper place, in its fitting order?

K: Of course. So is a human being afraid of all this? Unconsciously, deeply, he must realize the ending of me. Do you understand? And that is really a most frightening thing. My knowledge, my books, my wife—the whole thing which thought has put together. And you are asking me to end all that.

B: Can't you say it is the ending of everything? Because everything that I know is there.

K: Absolutely. So you see, really I am frightened; a human being is frightened of death. Not the biological death . . .

S: To die now.

K: This coming to an end. And therefore he believes in God, reincarnation, and a dozen other comforting things, but in actuality, when thought realizes itself as movement and sees that movement has created the me, the divisions, the quarrels, the whole structure of this chaotic world—when thought realizes this, sees the truth of it, it ends. Then there is cosmos. You listen to this: how do you receive it?

S: Do you want me to answer?

K: I offer you something. How do you receive it? This is very important.

S: Yes. Thought sees its movement . . .

K: No, no. How do you receive it? How does the public, who listens to all this, receive it? They ask, "What is he trying to tell me?"

S: What?

K: He says I am not telling you anything. He says listen to what I am saying and find out for yourself whether thought as movement has created all this, both the technological world which is useful, which is necessary, and this chaotic world.

S: Right.

K: How do you receive it, listen to it? What takes place in you when you listen to it?

S: Panic.

K: No. Is it?

S: Yes. There is a panic about the death. There is a sense of seeing, and then there is a fear of that death.

K: Which means you have listened to the words; the words have awakened the fear.

S: Right.

K: But not the actuality of the fact.

S: I wouldn't say that. I think that is a little unfair. They awaken the . . .

K: I am asking you.

S: . . . they awaken the actuality of the fact and then there seems to be a silence, a moment of great clarity that gives way to a kind of

76

feeling in the pit of the stomach where things are dropping out, and then there is a kind of . . .

K: Withholding.

S: . . . withholding, right. I think there is a whole movement there.

K: So you are describing humanity?

S: No I am describing me.

K: You are humanity.

B: You are the same.

S: Right.

K: You are the viewer, the people who are listening.

S: That's right. So there is a sense of what will happen tomorrow?

K: No, no. That is not the point. No. When thought realizes itself as a movement, and realizes that that movement has created all this chaos, total chaos, complete disorder—when it realizes that, what takes place? Actually? You are not frightened, there is no fear. Listen to it carefully. There is no fear. Fear is the idea brought about by an abstraction. You understand? You have made a picture of ending and are frightened of that ending.

S: You are right. You are right.

K: There is no fear.

S: No fear and then there is . . .

K: There is no fear when the actuality takes place.

S: That's right. When the actuality takes place there is silence.

K: With the fact there is no fear.

B: But as soon as thought comes in . . .

K: That's right.

S: That's right. Now wait a minute; no, don't go away. When thought comes in . . .

K: Then it is no longer a fact. You haven't remained with the fact.

B: Well, that is the same as saying you keep on thinking.

K: Keep on moving.

B: Yes. Well, as soon as you bring thought in, it is not a fact; it is an imagination or a fantasy which is thought to be real, but it is not so. Therefore you are not with the fact any longer.

K: We have discovered something extraordinary, that with fact there is no fear.

S: Right.

B: So all fear is thought, is that it?

K: That's right.

S: We have got a big mouthful here.

K: No. All thought is fear, all thought is sorrow.

B: That goes both ways, that all fear is thought, and all thought is fear.

K: Of course.

B: Except the kind of thought that arises with the fact alone.

S: I want to interject something right here: it seems to me we have discovered something quite important right here, which is that at the actual seeing, the instant of attention is at its peak.

K: No. Something new takes place, sir. Something totally new that you have never looked at. It has never been understood or experienced, whatever it is. A totally different thing happens.

B: But isn't it important that we acknowledge this in our thought, I mean in our language?

K: Yes.

B: As we are doing now. In other words, if it happened and we didn't acknowledge it, then we are liable to fall back.

K: Of course, of course.

S: I don't get you.

B: Well, we have to see it not only when it happens but we have to say that it happens.

S: Then are we creating a place to localize this, or not?

K: No, no. What he is saying is very simple. He is saying, does this fact, this actuality take place? And can you remain with it, can thought not move but remain only with that fact? Sir, it is like saying: Remain totally with sorrow. Do not move away, do not say it should be or shouldn't be, or how am I to get over it—just totally remain with that thing. With the fact. Then you have an energy which is extraordinary.

DIALOGUE V

May 19—afternoon

KRISHNAMURTI: We have talked about the necessity for human beings to change, and about why they don't change, why they accept this intolerable condition of the human psyche. I think we ought to approach the same thing from a different angle. Who has invented the unconscious?

Dr Shainberg: Who has invented it? I think there is a difference between what we *call* the unconscious and what *is* the unconscious. The word is not the thing.

K: Yes, the word is not the thing. Who has thought it up?

S: Well, I think the history of thinking about the unconscious is a long and involved process.

K: May we ask: Have you an unconscious? Are you aware of your unconscious? Do you know if you have an unconscious that is operating differently, trying to give you hints—are you aware of all that?

S: Yes. I am aware of an aspect of myself that is incompletely aware. That is what I call the unconscious. It is aware of my experience, aware of events in an incomplete way. That's what I call the unconscious. It uses symbols and different modes of telling, of understanding a dream, say, in which I discover jealousy that I wasn't aware of.

K: Do you also give importance, Dr Bohm, to a feeling that there is such a thing?

Dr Bohm: Well, I don't know what you mean by that. I think there are some things we do that we are not aware of. We react, we use words in an habitual way . . .

S: We have dreams.

B: We have dreams, yes . . .

K: I am going to question all that because I am not sure . . .

S: You are not questioning that we have dreams?

K: No. But I want to question, I want to ask the experts if there is such a thing as the unconscious, because I don't think it has played any important part in my life at all.

S: Well, it depends on what you mean.

K: I will tell you what I mean. Something hidden, something incomplete, something that I have to go after consciously or unconsciously—discover, unearth, explore and expose. See the motives, see the hidden intentions.

B: Well, could we make it clear that there are some things people do which you can see they are not aware of doing?

K: I don't quite follow.

B: Well, for example, this Freudian slip of the tongue—somebody makes a slip of the tongue which expresses his will.

K: Yes, yes, I didn't mean that quite.

S: That is what most people think of as the unconscious. You see, I think there are two problems here, if I can just put in a technical statement. There has arisen in the history of thinking about the unconscious, a belief that there are things in it which must be lifted out. Then there are a large group of people now who think of the unconscious as areas of behaviour, areas of response, areas of experience that they are not fully aware of, so that in the daytime they might have, let's say, an experience of stress which they didn't finish with, and at night they go through re-working it in a new way.

K: I understand all that.

S: So that would be the unconscious in operation. You get it also from the past or from previous programmes of action.

K: I mean—the collective unconscious, the racial unconscious.

B: Let's say somebody has been deeply hurt in the past; you can see that his whole behaviour is governed by that. But he doesn't know it; he may not know it.

K: Yes, that I understand.

S: But his response is always from the past.

80

K: Yes, quite. What I am trying to find out is why we have divided the conscious and the unconscious. Or is it one unitary total process—one movement? Not hidden, not concealed, but moving as a whole current. These clever brainy birds come along and split it up and say there is the conscious and the unconscious, the hidden, the incomplete, the storehouse of racial memories, family memories . . .

S: The reason that that has happened, I think, is partially explained by the fact that Freud and Jung and others were seeing patients who had fragmented off this movement which you are talking about. So much knowledge of the unconscious grew out of that.

K: That's what I want to get at.

S: There's the whole history of hysteria, where patients couldn't move their arms, you know?

K: I know.

S: Then you open up their memories and eventually they can move their arms. Or there were people who had dual personalities . . .

K: Is it an insanity—not insanity—is it a state of mind that divides everything, that says there is the unconscious and the conscious? Is it also a process of fragmentation?

B: Well, wouldn't you say, as Freud has said, that certain material is made unconscious by the brain because it is too disturbing?

K: That is what I want to get at.

B: It is fragmented. That is well known in all schools of psychology.

S: That's right. That is what I am saying. It is fragmented off and is then called the unconscious. What is fragmented is the unconscious.

K: I understand that.

B: But would you say that the brain itself is in some sense holding it separate on purpose in order to avoid it?

K: Yes, avoiding facing the fact.

S: That's right.

81

B: Yes. So that it is not really separate from consciousness.

K: That is what I want to get at.

S: It isn't separate from consciousness but the brain has organized it in a fragmented way.

B: Yes, but then it is a wrong terminology to call it that. The word unconscious already implies a separation.

K: That's right, separation.

B: To say there are two layers, the unconscious and the surface consciousness, a structure is implied. But this other notion is to say that that structure is not implied, but that certain material wherever it may be is simply avoided.

K: I don't want to think about somebody because he has hurt me. That is not the unconscious, it's just that I don't want to think about him.

S: That's right.

K: I am conscious he has hurt me and I don't want to think about it.

B: But a kind of paradoxical situation arises there because eventually you would become so good at it that you wouldn't realize you were doing it. That seems to happen, you see.

K: Yes, yes.

B: People become so proficient at avoiding these things that they cease to realize they are doing it.

K: Yes.

B: It becomes habitual.

S: That is right. I think this is what happens. These hurts . . .

K: The wound remains.

S: The wound remains and we forget that we have forgotten.

K: The wound remains.

B: We remember to forget, you see!

K: Yes.

S: We remember to forget and then the process of therapy is to help the remembering and the recall—to remember you have forgotten, and then to understand the connections of why you

82

forgot; then the thing can move in a more holistic way, rather than being fragmented.

K: Do you consider, or feel that you have been hurt?

S: Yes.

K: And want to avoid it? Resist, withdraw, isolate—the whole picture being the image of yourself being hurt and withdrawing—do you feel that when you are hurt?

S: Yes. I feel—how to put it?

K: Let's go into this.

S: Yes, I feel there is definitely a move not to be hurt, not to have that image, not to have that whole thing changed because if it is changed it seems to catapult into the same experience that was the hurt. This has a resonation with that unconscious which reminds me . . . you see I am reminded of being hurt deeply by this more superficial hurt.

K: I understand that.

S: So I avoid hurt—period.

K: If the brain has a shock—a biological, physical shock—must the psychological brain, if we can call it that, be hurt also? Is that inevitable?

S: No, I don't think so. It is only hurt with reference to something.

K: No. I am asking you: Can such a psychological brain, if I can use those two words, never be hurt?—in any circumstances, given family life, husband, wife, bad friends, so-called enemies, all that is going on around you—never get hurt? Because apparently this is one of the major wounds of human existence. The more sensitive you are, the more aware, the more hurt you get, the more withdrawn. Is this inevitable?

S: I don't think it is inevitable but I think it happens frequently, more often than not. And it seems to happen when an attachment is formed and then the loss of that attachment. You become important to me, I like you, or I am involved with you, then it becomes important to me that you don't do anything that disturbs that image.

K: That is, the relationship between two people, the picture we have of each other, the image—that is the cause of hurt.

B: Well, it also goes the other way: we hold those images because of hurt.

K: Of course, of course.

B: Where does it start?

K: That is what I want to get at.

S: That is what I want to get at too.

K: He pointed out something.

S: I know he did, yes.

B: Because the past hurt gives tremendous strength to the image, the image which helps us to forget it.

S: That's right.

K: Now is this wound in the "unconscious"—we use the word unconscious in quotes for the time being—is it hidden?

S: Well, I think you are being a little simplistic about that because what is hidden is the fact that I have had this happen many times—it happened with my mother, it happened with my friend, it happened in school, when I cared about somebody . . . You form the attachment and then comes the hurt.

K: I am not at all sure that it comes through attachment.

S: Maybe it is not attachment, that is the wrong word. What happens is that I form a relationship with you where an image becomes important—what you do to me becomes important.

K: You have an image about yourself.

S: That's right. And you are saying that I like you because you are conforming with the image.

K: No, apart from like and dislike, you have an image about yourself. Then I come along and put a pin in that image.

S: No, first you come along and confirm it.

B: The hurt will be greater if you first come along and are very friendly to me and confirm the image, and then suddenly put a pin in me.

K: Of course, of course.

B: But even somebody who didn't confirm it can hurt if he puts the pin in properly.

S: That's right. That's not unconscious. But why did I have the image to begin with? That is unconscious.

K: Is it unconscious? That is what I want to get at. Or it is so obvious that we don't look. You follow what I am saying?

S: I follow, yes.

K: We put it away. We say it is hidden. I question whether it is hidden at all, it is so blatantly obvious.

S: I don't feel all parts of it are obvious.

B: I think we hide it in one sense. Shall we say that this hurt means that everything is wrong with the image, but we hide it by saying everything is all right? In other words the thing that is obvious may be hidden by saying it is unimportant, that we don't notice it.

S: Yes, we don't notice it but I ask myself what is it that generates this image, what is that hurt?

K: Ah, we will come to that. We are enquiring, aren't we, into the whole structure of consciousness?

S: Right.

K: Into the nature of consciousness. We have broken it up into the hidden and the open. It may be the fragmented mind that is doing this. And therefore strengthening both.

S: Right.

K: The division grows greater and greater and greater . . .

S: The fragmented mind is . . .

K: . . . doing this. Now most people have an image about themselves, practically everybody. It is that image that gets hurt. And that image is you, and you say, "I am hurt".

B: It is the same as what we were discussing this morning.

K: Yes.

B: You see, if I have a pleasant self-image, I attribute the pleasure to me and say that it is real. When somebody hurts me then the pain is attributed to me and I say that's real too. It seems that if you have an image that can give you pleasure, then it must also be able to give you pain. There is no way out of that.

K: Absolutely.

85

S: Well, the image seems to be self-perpetuating, as you were saying.

B: I think people hope that the image will give them pleasure.

K: Pleasure only.

B: Only pleasure, but the very mechanism that makes pleasure possible makes pain possible, because the pleasure comes if I say "I think I am good", and this is sensed to be real, which makes that goodness real, but if somebody comes along and says, "You are no good, you are stupid", that too is real and therefore very significant.

K: The image brings both pleasure and pain.

B: I think people would hope for an image that would bring only pleasure.

S: People do hope that, there is no question. But people not only hope for the image, they invest all their interest in their image.

B: The value of everything depends on this self-image being right. So if somebody shows it's wrong, everything is wrong.

S: That's right.

K: But we are always giving new shape to the image.

B: But I think this image means everything, and that gives it tremendous power.

S: The entire personality is directed to the achievement of this image. Everything else takes second place.

K: Are you aware of this?

S: Yes. I am aware of it.

K: What is the beginning of this?

S: Well . . .

K: Please, just let me summarize first. Every human being practically has an image of himself, of which he is unconscious or not aware.

S: That's right. Usually it's sort of idealized.

K: Idealized, or not idealized, it is an image.

S: That's right. They must have it.

K: That have it.

B: They have it.

S: But they must direct all their actions towards getting it.

B: I think one feels one's whole life depends on the image.

K: Yes, that's right.

S: Depression is when I don't have it.

K: We will come to that. The next question is: How does it come into being?

S: Well, I think it comes into being in the family in some way. You are my father and I understand through watching you that if I am smart you will like me, right?

K: Quite. We agree.

S: I learn that very quickly. So I am going to make sure I get that love . . .

K: It is all very simple. But I am asking: What is the origin of making images about oneself?

B: If I had no image at all I would never get into that, would I?

S: If I never made images . . .?

B: Yes. Never made any image at all no matter what my father did.

K: I think this is very important.

S: That is the question.

B: Maybe the child can't do it, but suppose he can . . .

K: I am not at all sure . . .

B: Perhaps he can, but I am saying under ordinary conditions he doesn't manage to do it.

S: You are suggesting that the child already has an image that he has been hurt.

K: Ah, no, no. I don't know. We are asking.

B: But suppose there was a child who made no image of himself.

S: OK. Let's assume he has no image.

B: Then he cannot get hurt.

K: He can't be hurt.

S: There I think you are in very hot water psychologically because a child . . .

K: No, we said "suppose".

B: Not the actual child—but suppose there was a child who didn't make an image of himself so he didn't depend on that image for everything. The child you talked about depended on the image that his father loves him.

S: That's right.

B: And therefore when his father doesn't love him, everything has gone, right?

S: Right.

B: Therefore he is hurt. But if he has no image that he must have his father love him, then he will just watch his father.

S: But let's look at it a little more pragmatically. Here is the child and he is actually hurt.

B: He can't be hurt without the image. Who is going to get hurt?

K: It is like putting a pin into the air.

S: Now wait a minute, I am not going to let you guys get away with this! Here you have got this child vulnerable in the sense that he needs psychological support. He has enormous tensions.

K: Sir, agreed to all that. Such a child has an image.

S: No, no image. He is simply not being biologically supported.

K: No. No.

B: Well, he may make an image of the fact that he is not biologically supported. You have to get the difference between the actual fact of what happens biologically and what he thinks of it. Right? Now I have seen a child sometimes drop suddenly, he really goes to pieces, not because he was dropped very far but because that sense of . . .

K: Loss, insecurity.

B: . . . insecurity, because his mother was gone. It seemed as if everything had gone, right? And he was totally disorganized and screaming, but he dropped only about this far, you see. But the point is he had an image of the kind of security he was going to get from his mother. Right?

S: That is the way the nervous system works.

B: Well, that is the question—Is it necessary to work that way? Or is this the result of conditioning?

K: This is an important question.

S: Oh, terribly important.

K: Because whether in America or in this country, children are running away from their parents. The parents seem to have no control over them. They don't obey, they don't listen. They are wild. And the parents feel terribly hurt. I saw on TV what is happening in America. One woman was in tears. She said, "I am his mother, he doesn't treat me as a mother, he just orders me about." He had run away half a dozen times. And this separation between parents and children is growing all over the world. They have no relationship between themselves, between each other. So what is the cause of all this, apart from sociological, economic pressures which made the mother go out to work and leave the child alone—we take that for granted—but much deeper than that? Is it that the parents have an image about themselves and insist on creating an image in the children?

S: I see what you are saying.

K: And the child refuses to have that image—he has his own image. So the battle is on.

S: That is very much what I was saying when I said that initially the hurt of the child . . .

K: We haven't come to the hurt yet.

S: Well, what is in that initial relationship between child . . .

K: I doubt if they have any relationship. That is what I am trying to get at.

S: I agree with you. There is something wrong with the relationship.

K: Have they a relationship at all? Look, young people get married, or they don't get married. They have a child by mistake, or intentionally, but young people are children themselves; they haven't understood the universe, cosmos or chaos—they just have this child.

S: That's right. That is what happens.

K: And they play with it for a year or two and then say, "For God's sake, I am fed up with this child", and look elsewhere. And the child feels left, lost.

S: That's right.

K: And he needs security, from the beginning he needs security.

S: Right.

K: Which the parents do not give, or are incapable of giving—psychological security, the sense of "You are my child, I love you, I'll look after you, I'll see that throughout life you will behave properly". They haven't got that feeling. They are bored with it after a couple of years.

S: That's right.

K: Is it that they have no relationship right from the beginning, neither the husband, nor the wife, boy or girl? Is it only a sexual relationship, the pleasure relationship? Is it that they won't accept the pain principle involved with the pleasure principle?

S: That's right.

K: What I am trying to see is if there is actually any relationship at all, except a biological, sexual, sensual relationship.

S: Well . . .

K: I am questioning it, I am not saying it is so, I am questioning it.

S: I don't think it is so. I think they have a relationship but it is a wrong relationship.

K: There is no wrong relationship. It is a relationship or no relationship.

S: Well, then we will have to say they have a relationship. I think most parents have a relationship with their children.

B: Suppose the parent and child have images of each other, and the relationship is governed by those images—the question is whether that is actually a relationship or not, or whether it is some sort of fantasy of relationship.

K: A fanciful relationship. Sir, you have children—forgive me if I come back to you—you have children. Have you any relationship with them? In the real sense of that word.

S: Yes. In the real sense, yes.

K: That means you have no image about yourself.

S: Right.

K: And you are not imposing an image on them?

S: That's right.

K: And the society is not imposing an image on them?

S: There are moments like that . . .

K: Ah, no. That is not good enough. It is like a rotten egg.

S: This is an important point.

B: If it is moments it is not so. It is like saying a person who is hurt has moments when he is not hurt, but he is sitting there waiting to explode when something happens. So he can't go very far. It is like somebody who is tied to a rope, and as soon as he reaches the limits of that rope he is stuck.

S: That is right.

B: So you could say I am related as long as certain things are all right, but beyond that point it just sort of blows up. You see what I am driving at? That mechanism is inside there, buried, so it dominates me potentially. It is like the man who is tied to a rope and says there are moments when I can move wherever I like, but I can't really because if I keep on moving I am bound to come to the end.

S: That does seem to be what happens, in fact. There is a reverberation in which there is a yank-back.

B: Either I come to the end of the cord, or else something yanks the cord. The person who is on the end of a cord is really not free ever.

S: Well, that's true, I mean I think that is true.

B: You see in the same sense the person who has the image is not really related ever.

K: Yes, that is just the whole point. You can play with it verbally, but the actuality is that you have no relationship.

S: You have no relationship as long as it is the image.

K: As long as you have an image about yourself you have no relationship with another. This is a tremendous revelation—you follow? It is not just an intellectual statement.

S: I have the memory of times when I do have what I think is a relationship, yet one must be honest with you, and say that after such relationship there inevitably seems to be this yank-back. •

B: The end of the cord.

S: Yes, a yank-back. You have a relationship with somebody but you will go just so far.

K: Of course. That is understood.

B: But then really the image controls it all the time because the image is the dominant factor. If you once pass that point, no matter what happens, the image takes over.

K: So the image gets hurt, and the child, because you impose the image on the child. You are bound to because you have an image. Because you have an image about yourself you are bound to create an image in the child.

S: That is right.

K: You follow, you have discovered? And society is doing this to all of us.

B: So you say the child is picking up an image just naturally, as it were, quietly, and then suddenly it is hurt?.

K: Hurt. That's right.

B: So the hurt has been prepared and preceded by this steady process of building an image?

S: That's right. There is evidence, for instance, that we treat boys differently from girls . . .

K: No. Look at it: don't verbalize it too quickly.

B: You see, if the steady process of building an image didn't occur there would be no basis, no structure, to get hurt. In other words the pain is due entirely to some psychological fact. Whereas I was previously enjoying the pleasure of saying, "My father loves me, I am doing what he wants"—now comes the pain—"I am not doing what he wants, he doesn't love me".

S: I don't think we touched on the biological situation of the child feeling neglected.

B: Well, if the child is neglected, he must pick up an image in that very process.

92

K: Of course. If you admit, see it as a reality, that as long as the parents have an image about themselves they are bound to give that image to the child . . .

S: Right. There is no question, as long as the parent is the image-maker and has an image, he can't see the child.

K: And therefore gives an image to the child.

S: Right. He will condition the child to be something.

K: You see, society is doing this to every human being. Religions, every culture around us is creating this image. And that image gets hurt. Now the next question is: Is one aware of all this? Which is part of our consciousness.

S: Right, right.

K: The content of consciousness makes up consciousness. That is clear.

S: Right.

K: So one of the contents is the image-making, or maybe the major machinery that is operating, the major dynamo, the major movement. Being hurt, which every human being is—can that hurt be healed and never be hurt again? That is, can a human mind which has created the image, which has accepted the image, can that mind put away the image completely and never be hurt?—which means that a great part of consciousness is empty—it has no content. I wonder.

S: Can it? I really don't know the answer to that.

K: Why? Who is the image-maker? What is the machinery or the process that is making images? I may get rid of one image and take on another. I am a Catholic, I am a Protestant, I am a Hindu, I am a Zen monk, I am this, I am that—you follow?—they are all images.

S: Who is the image-maker?

K: You see, after all, if there is an image of that kind how can you have love in all this?

S: We don't have an abundance of it.

K: We don't have it.

S: That's right. We have got a lot of images. That is why I say I don't know.

K: It is terrible, sir, to have these images—you follow?

S: Right. I know about image-making, I see it. I see it even when you are talking about it. I can see that if I don't make one image I will make another.

K: Of course, sir. We are saying, Is it possible to stop the machinery that is producing images? And what is the machinery? Is it wanting to be somebody?

S: Yes. It is wanting to be somebody, it is wanting to know—wanting to have. Somehow or other it seems to be wanting to handle the feeling that if I don't have it I don't know where I am.

K: Being at a loss?

S: Yes. The feeling that you are at a loss. Not to be able to rely on anything, not to have any support, breeds more disorder—you follow?

B: That is one of the images . . .

K: The image is the product of thought—right?

S: It is organized.

K: Yes, a product of thought. It may go through various forms of pressure, a great deal of conveyor belt, and at the end it produces an image.

S: Right. No question. I agree with you there, yes.

K: Can the machinery stop? Can thought which produces these images, which destroys all relationship so that there is no love—not verbally but actually no love—can it stop? When a man who has got an image about himself says, "I love my wife, or my children", it is just sentiment, romantic, fanciful emotionalism.

S: Right.

K: As it is now, there is no love in the world. There is no sense of real caring for somebody.

S: That is true.

K: The more affluent the worse it becomes. Not that the poor have this. I don't mean that. Poor people haven't got this either—they are concerned with filling their stomachs, and work, work, work.

B: But still they have got lots of images.

K: Of course. All these are the people who are correcting the

94

world—right? Who are ordering the universe. So I ask myself, can this image-making stop? Stop, not occasionally, but stop. Because unless it does I don't know what love means. I don't know how to care for somebody. And I think that is what is happening in the world because children are really lost souls, lost human beings. I have met so many, hundreds of them now, all over the world. They are really a lost generation. As the older people are a lost generation. So what is a human being to do? What is the right action in relationship? Can there be right action in relationship as long as you have an image?

S: No.

K: Ah! Sir, this is something tremendous.

S: That is why I was wondering. It seemed to me you made a jump there. You said all we know is images, and image-making. That is all we know.

K: But we never said can it stop?

S: We have never said can it stop—that is right.

K: We have never said, for God's sake if it doesn't stop we are going to destroy each other.

B: You could say that the notion we might stop is something more we know that we didn't know before . . .

K: It becomes another piece of knowledge.

B: I was trying to say that when you say "all we know", a block comes in.

S: Right.

B: You see, it is not much use to say "all we know". If you say it is all we know then it can never stop.

K: He is objecting to your use of "all".

S: I am grateful to you.

B: That is one of the factors blocking it.

S: Well, if we come down to it, what do we do with that question: Can it stop?

K: I put that question to you. Do you listen to it?

S: I listen to it—right.

K: Ah, do you?

S: It stops.

K: No, no. I am not interested in whether it stops. Do you listen to the question, Can it stop? We now examine, analyse, this whole process of image-making—the result of it, the misery, the confusion, the appalling things that are going on. The Arab has his image, the Jew, the Hindu, the Muslim, the Christian, the Communist. There is this tremendous division of images, of symbols. If that doesn't stop, you are going to have such a chaotic world—you follow?—I see this, not as an abstraction, but as an actuality, as I see that flower.

S: Right.

K: And as a human being, what am I to do? Because I personally have no image about this. I really mean I have no image about myself, no conclusion, no concept, no ideal—none of these images. I have none. And I say to myself what can I do?—when everybody around me is building images and so destroying this lovely earth where we are meant to live happily in human relationship and look at the heavens and be happy about it. So what is the right action for a man who has an image? Or is there no right action?

S: Let me turn it back. What happens with you when I say to you: Can it stop?

K: I say, of course. It is very simple to me. Of course it can stop. You don't ask me the next question: How do you do it? How does it come about?

S: No, I just want to listen for a minute to when you say, "Yes, of course". OK. Now how do you think it can stop? Let me put it to you straight—I have absolutely no evidence that it can, no experience that it can.

K: I don't want evidence.

S: You don't want any evidence?

K: I don't want somebody's explanation.

S: Or experience?

K: Because they are based on images. Future image, or past image or living image. So I say: Can it stop? I say it can. Definitely. It is not just a verbal statement to amuse you. To me this is tremendously important.

S: Well, I think we agree that it is tremendously important, but how?

K: Not how. Then you enter into the question of systems, mechanical processes, which are part of our image-making. If I tell you how, you will say tell me the system, the method and I'll do it every day and I'll get the new image.

S: Yes.

K: Now I see the fact of what is going on in the world.

S: I am with you, yes.

K: Fact. Not my reaction to it. Not romantic, fanciful theories of what it should not be. It is a fact that as long as there are images there is not going to be peace in the world, or love in the world—whether it be the Christ image, or the Buddha image or the Muslim image—you follow? There won't be peace in the world. Right. I see it as a fact. Right? I remain with that fact. Finished. This morning we said that if one remains with the fact there is a transformation. That is, not let thought interfere with the fact.

B: For then more images come in.

K: More images come in. So our consciousness is filled with these images.

S: Yes, that is true.

K: I am a Hindu, a Brahmin, I am by tradition better than anybody else, I am the chosen people, I am the Aryan—you follow? I am an Englishman—all that is crowding my consciousness.

B: When you say remain with the fact, one of the images that may come in is that it is impossible, that it can never be done.

K: Yes, that is another image.

B: In other words, if the mind could stay with that fact with no comment whatsoever . . .

S: The thing that comes through to me when you say remain with the fact is that you are really calling for an action right there.

K: Sir, it is up to you. You are involved in it.

S: But that is different from remaining with it.

K: Remain with that.

97

S: To really see it. You know how that feels? It feels like we are always running away.

K: So our consciousness, sir, is these images—conclusions, ideas . . .

S: We are always running away.

K: Filling, filling, and that is the essence of the image. If there is no image-making what is consciousness? That is quite a different thing.

B: Do you think we could discuss that next time?

K: Yes. Tomorrow.

DIALOGUE VI

May 20—morning

KRISHNAMURTI: Dr Bohm, as you are a well-known physicist, I would like to ask you, after these five dialogues we have had, what will change man? What will bring about a radical transformation in the total consciousness of human beings?

Dr Bohm: Well, I don't know that the scientific background is very relevant to that question.

K: No, probably not, but after having talked together at length, not only now but in previous years, what is the energy—I am using energy not in any scientific sense but in the just ordinary sense—the vitality, the energy, the drive—which seems to be lacking? If I were listening to the three of us, if I were a viewer, I would say, "Yes, it is all very well for these philosophers, these scientists, these experts, but it is outside my field. It is too far away. Bring it nearer. Bring it much closer so that I can deal with my life."

B: Well, I think at the end of the last discussion we were touching on one point of that nature, because we were discussing images.

K: Images, yes.

B: And the self-image. And questioning whether we have to have images at all.

K: Of course, we went into that. But, you see, as a viewer, totally outside, listening to you for the first time, the three of you, I would say, "How does it touch my life? It is all so vague and uncertain and it needs a great deal of thinking, which I am unwilling to do. So please tell me in a few words, or at length, what am I to do with my life. Where am I to touch it? Where am I to break it down? From where am I to look at it? I have hardly any time. I go to the office. I go to the factory. I have got so many things to do—children, a nagging wife, poverty—the whole structure of misery, and you sit there, you three, and talk about something which doesn't touch me in the least. So could we bring it down to brass tacks, as it were, where I can grapple with it as an ordinary being?"

B: Well, could we consider problems arising in daily relationship as the starting point?

K: That is the essence, isn't it? I was going to begin with that. You see, my relationship with human beings is in the office, in the factory, on a golf-course.

B: Or at home.

K: Or at home. And at home there is routine, sex, children (if I have children, if I want children), and the constant battle, battle, battle all my life. Insulted, wounded, hurt—everything is going on in me and around me.

B: Yes, there is continual disappointment.

K: Continual disappointment, continual hope, desire to be more successful, to have more money—more, more, more of everything. Now how am I to change my relationship? What is the *raison d'être*, the source of my relationship? If we could tackle that a little bit this morning, and then go on to what we were discussing, which was really much more—which is really very important—which is not to have an image at all.

B: Yes. But it seems, as we were discussing yesterday, that we tend to be related almost always through the image.

K: Through the image. That's right.

B: You see I have an image of myself and of you as you should be in relation to me.

K: Yes.

B: And then that gets disappointed and hurt and so on.

K: But how am I to change that image? How am I to break it down? I see very well that I have got an image and that it has been put together, constructed, through generations. I am fairly intelligent, I am fairly aware of myself, and I see I have got it. But how am I to break it down?

B: Well, as I see it, I have got to be aware of that image, watch it as it moves.

K: So I am to watch it? Am I to watch it in the office?

B: Yes.

100

K: In the factory, at home, on the golf-course?—because my relationships are in all these areas.

B: Yes, I would say I have to watch it in all those places.

K: I have to watch it all the time in fact.

B: Yes.

K: Now am I capable of it? Have I got the energy? I go through all kinds of miseries, and at the end of the day I crawl into bed. And you say I must have energy. So I must realize that relationship is of the greatest importance.

B: Yes.

K: Therefore I am willing to give up certain wastages of energy.

B: What kind of wastage?

K: Drinking, smoking, useless chatter. Endless crawling from pub to pub.

B: That would be the beginning, anyway.

K: That would be the beginning. But you see I want all those, plus more—you follow?

B: But if I can see that everything depends on this . . .

K: Of course.

B: . . . then I won't go to the pub, if I see it interferes.

K: So I must, as an ordinary human being, realize that the greatest importance is to have right relationship.

B: Yes. It would be good if we could say what happens when we don't have it.

K: Oh, when I don't have it, of course . . .

B: Everything goes to pieces.

K: Not only everything goes to pieces but I create such havoc around me. So can I, by putting aside smoke, drink, and endless chatter about this or that—can I gather that energy? Will I gather that energy which will help me to face the picture which I have, the image which I have?

B: That means going into ambition also and many other things.

K: Of course. You see I begin by obvious things, like smoking, drinking, the pub . . .

Dr Shainberg: Let me just stop you here. Suppose my real image is that you are going to do it for me, that I can't do it for myself.

K: That is one of our favourite conditionings—that I can't do it myself, therefore I must go to somebody to help me.

S: Or I go to the pub because I am in despair because I can't do it for myself and want to obliterate myself through drink, so that I no longer feel the pain of it.

B: At least for the moment.

S: That's right. And also I am proving to myself that my image that I can't do it for myself is right. By treating myself in such a way I am going to prove to you that I can't do it for myself, so maybe you will do it for me.

K: No, no. I think we don't realize, any of us, the utter and absolute importance of right relationship. I don't think we realize it.

S: I agree with you. We don't.

K: With my wife, with my neighbour, with the office, wherever I am—and also with nature—I don't think we realize a relationship which is easy, quiet, full, rich, happy—the beauty of it, the harmony of it. Now can we tell the ordinary viewer, the listener, the great importance of that?

S: Let's try. How can we communicate to somebody the value of a right relationship? You are my wife. You are whining, nagging me—right? You think I should be doing something for you when I am tired and don't feel like doing anything for you.

K: I know. Go to a party.

S: That's right. "Let's go to a party. You never take me out. You never take me anywhere."

K: So how are you, who realize the importance of relationship, to deal with me? How? We have got this problem in life.

B: I think it should be very clear that nobody can do it for me. Whatever somebody else does won't affect my relationship.

S: How are you going to make that clear?

B: But isn't it clear?

S: It is not obvious. I, as the viewer, feel very strongly that you ought to be doing it for me. My mother never did it for me, somebody has got to do it for me.

B: But isn't it obvious that it can't be done? It is just a delusion because whatever you do I will be in the same relationship as before. Suppose you live a perfect life. I can't imitate it, so I'll just go on as before, won't I? So I have to do something for myself. Isn't that clear?

S: But I don't feel able to do anything for myself.

B: But can't you see that if you don't do anything for yourself it is inevitable that it must go on? Any idea that it will ever get better is a delusion.

S: Can we say then that right relationship begins with the realization that I have to do something for myself?

K: And the utter importance of it.

S: Right. The utter importance. The responsibility I have for myself.

K: Because you are the world. And the world is you. You can't shirk that.

B: Perhaps we could discuss that a bit because it may seem strange to the viewer to hear someone say "You are the world".

K: After all, you are the result of the culture, the climate, the food, the environment, the economic conditions, your grand-parents—you are the result of all that—all your thinking is the result of that.

S: I think you can see that.

B: That's right. That's what you mean by saying you are the world.

K: Of course, of course.

S: Well I think you can see that in what I have been saying about the person who feels he is entitled to be taken care of by the world—the world is in fact moving in that direction . . .

K: No, sir. This is a fact. You go to India, you see the same suffering, the same anxiety—and you come to Europe, to America, and in essence it is the same.

B: Each person has the same basic structure of suffering and confusion and deception. Therefore if I say I am the world, I mean that there is a universal structure and it is part of me and I am part of that.

K: Part of that, quite. So now let's proceed from there. The first thing you have to tell me as an ordinary human being, living in this mad rat race, is, "Look, realize that the greatest, most important thing in life is relationship. You cannot have relationship if you have an image about yourself. Any form of image you have about another, or about yourself, prevents the beauty of relationship."

S: Right.

B: Yes. The image that I am secure in such and such a relation, for example, and not secure in a different situation, prevents relationship.

K: That's right.

B: Because I will demand of the other person that he put me in the situation that I think is secure, you see?

S: Right.

B: But he may not want to.

S: Right. So that if I have the image of a pleasurable relationship, I have what I call claims on the other person; in other words I expect him to act in such a way that he acknowledges that image.

B: Yes. Or I may say that I have the image of what is just and right.

S: In order to complete my image?

B: Yes. For example, the wife says, "Husbands should take their wives out to parties frequently"—that is part of the image. Husbands have corresponding images and then those images get hurt.

S: I think we have to be very specific about this. Each little piece of this is with fury.

B: With energy.

S: Energy and fury and the necessity to complete this image in relationship; therefore relationship gets forced into a mould.

K: Sir, I understand all that. But you see most of us are not serious. We want an easy life. You come along and tell me: relationship is the greatest thing. I say, of course, quite right. And I carry on in the old way. What I am trying to get at is this: What will make a human being listen to this seriously even for two minutes? He won't listen to it. If you went to one of the great experts on psychology, or whatever it is, he wouldn't take time to listen to it.

The experts have all got their own plans, their pictures, their images—they are surrounded by all this. So to whom are we talking?

B: To whoever can listen.

S: We are talking to ourselves.

K: No. Not only that. To whom are we talking?

B: Well, whoever is able to listen.

K: That means somebody who is somewhat serious.

B: Yes. And I think we may even form an image of ourselves as not capable of being serious.

K: That's right.

B: In other words that it is too hard.

K: Too hard, yes.

B: There is an image to say I want it easy, which comes from the image that this is beyond my capacity.

K: Quite. So let's move from there. We say that as long as you have an image, pleasant or unpleasant, created, put together by thought, there is no right relationship. That is an obvious fact. Right?

S: Right.

B: Yes, and life ceases to have any value without right relationship.

K: Yes, life ceases to have any value without right relationship. Now my consciousness is filled with these images. Right? And the images make my consciousness.

S: That is right.

K: Now you are asking me to have no images at all. That means no consciousness, as I know it now. Right, sir?

B: Yes, well could we say that the major part of consciousness is the self-image? There may be some other parts but . . .

K: We will come to that.

B: We come to that later. But for now, we are mostly occupied with the self-image.

K: Yes. That is right.

105

S: What about the self-image? And the whole way it generates itself?

B: We discussed that before. It gets caught on thinking of the self as real. That is always implicit. Say, for example, the image may be that I am suffering in a certain way, and I must get rid of this suffering. There is always the implicit meaning in that that I am real, and therefore I must keep on thinking about this reality. And it gets caught in that feedback we were talking about—the thought feeds back and builds up.

S: Builds up more images.

B: More images, yes.

S: So that is the consciousness . . .

K: Wait. The content of my consciousness is a vast series of images, inter-related—not separated, but inter-related.

B: But they are all centred on the self.

K: On the self, of course. The self is the centre.

B: The self is regarded as all important.

K: Yes.

B: That gives it tremendous energy.

K: Now what I am getting at is this: you are asking me, who am fairly serious, fairly intelligent, asking me as an ordinary human being to empty that consciousness.

S: Right. I am asking you to stop this image-making.

K: Not only the image-making. You are asking me to be free of the self, which is the maker of images.

S: Right.

K: And I say please tell me how to do it. And you tell me that the moment you ask me how to do it, you are already building an image, a system, a method.

B: Yes, when you ask how am I to do it—you have already put 'I' in the middle. The same image as before with a slightly different content.

K: So you tell me, never to ask how to do it because the "how" involves the me doing it. Therefore I am creating another picture.

B: That shows the way you slip into it. When you ask how to do it, the word "me" is not there but it is there implicitly.

K: Implicitly, yes.

B: And therefore you slip in.

K: So now you stop me and say proceed from there. What is the action that will free consciousness, even a corner of it, a limited part of it? I want to discuss it with you. Don't tell me how to do it. I have understood that and I will never again ask how to do it. The how, as Dr Bohm explained, conveys implicitly the me wanting to do it, and the me is the factor of the image-maker.

S: Right.

K: I have understood that very clearly. So then I say to you, I realize this—what am I to do?

S: Do you realize it?

K: Yes, sir. I know it. I know I am making images all the time. I am very well aware of it. Because I have discussed with you. I have gone into it. I have realized right from the beginning during these talks that relationship is the most important thing in life. Without that life is chaos.

S: Got it.

K: That has been driven into me. I see that every flattery and every insult is registered in the brain, and that thought then takes it over as memory and creates an image, and the image gets hurt.

B: So the image is the hurt . . .

K: . . . is the hurt.

S: That's right.

K: So, Dr Bohm, what is one to do? What am I to do? There are two things involved in it—one is to prevent further hurts and the other is to be free of all the hurts that I have had.

B: But they are both the same principle.

K: I think there are two principles involved.

B: Are there?

K: One to prevent it, the other to wipe away the hurts I have.

S: It is not just that I want to prevent the further hurt. It seems to me that you must first say how I am to be aware of how in fact I take flattery. I want you to see that if I flatter you, you get a big inner gush; then you get a fantasy about yourself. So now you have got an image of yourself as this wonderful person who fits the flattery.

K: No, you have told me very clearly that it is two sides of the same coin. Pleasure ·and pain are the same.

S: The same, exactly the same.

K: You have told me that.

S: That's right. I am telling you that.

K: I have understood it.

B: They are both images.

K: Both images, right. So please—you are not answering my question. How am I, realizing all this, I am a fairly intelligent man, I have read a great deal, an ordinary man—I personally don't read so it is an ordinary man I am talking about—I have discussed this and I see how extraordinarily important all this is—and I ask, how am I to end it? Not the method. Don't tell me what to do. I won't accept it because it means nothing to me—right, sirs?

B: Well, we were discussing whether there is a difference between the stored-up hurts and the ones which are to come.

K: That's right. It is the first thing I have to understand. Tell me.

B: Well, it seems to me that fundamentally they work on the same principle.

K: How?

B: Well, if you take the hurt that is to come my brain is already disposed to respond with an image.

K: I don't understand it. Make it much simpler.

B: Well, there is no distinction really between the past hurts and the present one because they all come from the past, I mean come from the reaction of the past.

K: So you are telling me, don't divide the past hurt from the future hurt because the image is the same.

B: Yes. The process is the same. I may just be reminded of the past hurt, and that is the same as somebody else insulting me.

K: Yes, yes. So you are saying to me, don't divide the past from the future hurt. There is only hurt. Therefore look at the image, not in

108

terms of past hurts or future hurts but just look at that image which is both the past and the future.

B: Yes.

K: Right?

B: But we are saying look at the image, not at its particular content but its general structure.

K: Yes, yes, that's right. Now then my next question is: How am I to look at it? Because I have already an image with which I am going to look. You promise me by your words, not promise exactly, but give me hope that if I have right relationship I will live a life that will be extraordinarily beautiful, I will know what love is—therefore I am already excited by this idea.

B: Then I have to be aware of an image of that kind too.

K: Yes, yes. Therefore, how am I—that is my point—how am I to look at this image? I know I have an image, not only one image but several images, but the centre of that image is me, the I—I know all that. Now how am I to look at it? May we proceed now? Right. Is the observer different from that which he is observing? That is the real question.

B: That is the question, yes. You could say that that is the root of the power of the image.

K: Yes, yes. You see, sir, what happens? If there is a difference between the observer and the observed there is that interval of time in which other activities go on.

B: Well, yes, in which the brain eases itself into something more pleasant.

K: Yes. And where there is a division there is conflict. So you are telling me to learn the art of observing, which is: that the observer is the observed.

B: Yes, but I think we could look first at our whole conditioning, which tells us that the observer is different from the observed.

K: Different. Of course.

B: We should perhaps look at that, because that is what everybody feels.

K: That the observer is different.

109

B: Ordinarily, when I am thinking of myself, that self is a reality, which is independent of thought, do you see?

K: Yes, we think that it is independent of thought.

B: And that the self is the observer who is a reality.

K: Quite right.

B: Who is independent of thought and who is thinking, who is producing thought.

K: But it is the product of thought.

B: Yes. That is the confusion.

K: Are you telling me, sir, that the observer is the result of the past?

B: Yes. One can see that.

K: My memories, my experiences—it is all the past.

B: Yes, but I think the viewer may find it a little hard to follow that, if he hasn't gone into it.

S: Very hard, I think.

K: Be fairly simple.

S: What do you mean?

K: Don't you live in the past? Your life is the past.

S: Right.

K: You are living in the past. Right?

S: That's right, yes.

K: Past memories, past experiences.

S: Yes, past memories, past becomings.

K: And from the past you project the future.

S: Right.

K: You hope that you will be good, that you will be different in future. It's always from the past to the future.

S: That's right. That's how it is lived.

K: Now that past is the me, of course.

B: But it does look as if it is something independent . . .

K: Is it independent?

B: It isn't, but . . .

K: I know, that is what we are asking. Is the me independent of the past?

B: It looks as if the me is here looking at the past.

K: The me is the product of the past.

S: Right. I can see that.

K: How do you see it?

B: Intellectually.

S: I see it intellectually.

K: Then you don't see it.

S: Right. That is what I am coming to.

K: You are playing tricks.

S: I see it as an intellectual—that's right, that's right. I see it intellectually.

K: Do you see this table intellectually?

S: No.

K: Why?

S: There is an immediacy of perception there.

K: Why isn't there an immediacy of perception of a truth, which is that you are the past?

S: Because time comes in. I imagine that I have gone through time.

K: What do you mean imagine?

S: I have an image of myself at three, I have an image of myself at ten and I have an image of myself at seventeen, and I say that they followed in sequence in time. I see myself having developed over that time. I am different now from what I was five years ago.

K: Are you?

S: I am telling you that that is how I have got that image. That image of a developmental sequence.

K: I understand all that, sir.

S: And I exist as a storehouse of memories, of accumulated incidents.

K: That is, time has produced that.

S: Right. I see that, right.

111

K: What is time?

S: I have just described it to you. Time is a movement . . . I have moved from the time I was three.

K: From the past, it is a movement.

S: That's right. From three to ten, to seventeen.

K: Yes, I understand. Now, is that movement an actuality?

S: What do you mean by actuality?

B: Or is it an image? Is it an image, or is it an actuality? I mean, if I have an image of myself as saying "I need this", it may not be an actual fact—right? It is just . . .

K: An image is not a fact.

S: Right. But I feel . . .

K: No, what you feel is like saying "my experience".

S: No, I am describing an actual . . .

B: But that is the whole point about the image, that it imitates an actual fact, you get the feeling that it is real. In other words I feel that I am really there—an actual fact looking at the past, at how I have developed.

S: Right.

B: But is it a fact that I am doing that?

S: What do you mean? It is an actual fact that I get the feeling that I am looking.

B: Yes, but is it an actual fact that that is the way it all is and was?

S: No, it is not. I can see the incorrectness of my memory which constructs me in time. I mean, obviously I was much more at three than I can remember; I was more at ten than I can remember, and obviously there was much more going on at seventeen than I have in my memory.

B: Yes, but the me who is here now is looking at all that.

S: That's right.

B: But is he really there and is he looking? That is the question.

S: Is the me that is looking . . .?

K: . . . an actuality. As this table is.

S: Well, let's . . .

112

K: Stick to it, stick to it.

S: That is what I am going to do. What is an actuality is this development, this image of a developmental sequence.

B: And the me who is looking at it?

S: And the me who is looking at it, that's right.

B: But it may be, in fact it is, that the me who is looking at it is also an image as is the developmental sequence.

S: You are saying then that this image of me is . . .

K: . . . is not reality.

B: It is not a reality independent of thinking.

K: So we must go back to find out what is reality.

S: Right.

K: Reality, we said, is everything that thought has put together. The table, the illusion, the churches, the nations—everything that thought has contrived is reality. But nature is not this sort of reality. It is not put together by thought, though it is nevertheless a reality.

B: It is a reality independent of thought. But is the me who is looking, a reality independent of thought, like nature?

K: That is the whole point. Have you understood?

S: Yes. I am beginning to see.

K: Sir, just let's be simple. We said we have images; I know I have images and you tell me to look at them, to be aware of them, to perceive the image. Is the perceiver different from the perceived? That is all my question is.

S: I know. I know.

K: Because if he is different then the whole process will go on indefinitely—right? But if there is no division, if the observer is the observed, then the whole problem changes.

S: Right.

K: Right? So is the observer different from the observed? Obviously not. So can I look at that image without the observer? And is there an image when there is no observer? Because the observer makes the image, the observer is the movement of thought.

113

B: We shouldn't call it the observer then because it is not looking. I think the language is confusing.

K: The language is, yes.

B: Because if you say it is an observer that implies that something is looking.

K: Yes, quite.

B: What you really mean is that thought is moving and creating an image as if it were looking, but nothing is being seen.

K: Yes.

B: Therefore there is no observer.

K: That is right. But put it round the other way: Is there a thinker without thought?

B: No.

K: Exactly. There you are. If there is no experiencer is there an experience? So you have asked me to look at my images, which is a very serious and very penetrating demand. You say look at them without the observer, because the observer is the image-maker, and if there is no observer, if there is no thinker, there is no thought—right? So there is no image. You have shown me something enormously significant.

S: As you said the question changes completely.

K: Completely. I have no image.

S: It feels completely different. It's as if there is a silence.

K: So I am saying, my consciousness is the consciousness of the world, because, in essence, it is filled with the things of thought—sorrow, fear, pleasure, despair, anxiety, attachment, hope;—it is a turmoil of confusion; a sense of deep agony is involved in it all. And in that state I cannot have any relationship with any human being.

S: Right.

K: So you say to me: To have the greatest and most responsible relationship is to have no image. You have pointed out to me that to be free of images, the maker of the image must be absent. The maker of the image is the past, is the observer who says "I like this", "I don't like this", who says "my wife, my husband, my house"—the me who is in essence the image. I have understood

114

this. Now the next question is: Are the images hidden so that I can't grapple with them, can't get hold of them? All you experts have told me that there are dozens of underground images—and I say, "By Jove, they must know, they know much more than I do, so I must accept what they say." But how am I to unearth them, expose them? You see, you have put me, the ordinary man, into a terrible position.

S: You don't have to unearth them once it is clear to you that the observer is the observed.

K: Therefore you are saying there is no unconscious.

S: Right.

K: You, the expert! You, who talk endlessly about the unconscious with your patients.

S: I don't.

K: You say there is no unconscious.

S: Right.

K: I agree with you. I say it is so. The moment you see that the observer is the observed, that the observer is the maker of images, it is finished.

S: Finished. Right.

K: Right through.

S: If you really see that.

K: That's it. So the consciousness which I know, in which I have lived, has undergone a tremendous transformation. Has it? Has it for you? And if I may ask Dr Bohm also—both of you, all of us—realizing that the observer is the observed, and that therefore the image-maker is no longer in existence, and so the content of consciousness, which makes up consciousness, is not as we know it—what then?

S: I don't know how you say it . . .

K: I am asking this question because it involves meditation. I am asking this question because all religious people, the really serious ones who have gone into this question, see that as long as we live our daily lives within the area of this consciousness—with all its images, and the image-maker—whatever we do will still be in that area. Right? One year I may become a Zen-Buddhist, and another year I may follow some guru, and so on and so on, but it is always within that area.

S: Right.

K: So what happens when there is no movement of thought, which is the image-making—what then takes place? You understand my question? When time, which is the movement of thought, ends, what is there? Because you have led me up to this point. I understand it very well. I have tried Zen meditation, I have tried Hindu meditation, I have tried all the kinds of other miserable practices and then I hear you, and I say, "By Jove, this is something extraordinary these people are saying. They say that the moment there is no image-maker, the content of consciousness undergoes a radical transformation and thought comes to an end, except in its right place." Thought comes to an end, time has a stop. What then? Is that death?

S: It is the death of the self.

K: No, no.

S: It is self-destruction.

K: No, no, sir. It is much more than that.

S: It is the end of something.

K: No, no. Just listen to it. When thought stops, when there is no image-maker, there is a complete transformation in consciousness because there is no anxiety, there is no fear, there is no pursuit of pleasure, there are none of the things that create turmoil and division. Then what comes into being, what happens? Not as an experience because that is out. What takes place? I have to find out, for you may be leading me up the wrong path!

DIALOGUE VII

May 20—afternoon

KRISHNAMURTI: After this morning, as an outsider, you have left me completely empty, without any future, without any past, without any image.

Dr Shainberg: That's right. Somebody who was watching us this morning said, "How am I going to get out of bed in the morning?"

K: I think that question of getting out of bed in the morning is fairly simple, because life demands that I act, not just stay in bed for the rest of my life. You see, I have been left, as an outsider who is viewing all this, who is listening to all this, with a sense of a blank wall. I understand what you have said very clearly. I have, at one glance, rejected all the systems, all the gurus, this meditation and that meditation. I have discarded all that because I have understood the meditator is the meditation. But have I solved my problem of sorrow, do I know what it means to love, do I understand what compassion is?—not just understand intellectually. At the end of these dialogues, after discussing with you all, listening to you all, have I this sense of astonishing energy which is compassion? Have I ended my sorrow? Do I know what it means to love somebody, to love human beings . . .?

S: Actually.

K: Actually.

S: . . . not just talk about it.

K: No, no, I have gone beyond all that. And you haven't shown me what death is.

Dr Bohm: No.

K: I haven't understood a thing about death. You haven't talked to me about death. So we will cover these things before we finish this evening.

B: Could we begin with the question of death?

K: Yes. Let's begin with death.

B: One point occurred to me about what we discussed this morning: We had come to the point of saying that when we see that the observer is the observed, that is death. Essentially that is what you said. Now this raises a question: If the self is nothing but an image what is it that dies? If the image dies that is nothing, it is not death—right?

K: That's right.

B: So is there something real that dies?

K: There is biological death.

B: We are not discussing that at the moment. You were discussing some other kind of death.

K: We were saying this morning, that if there are no images at all in my consciousness, there is death.

B: That is the point. It is not clear. What is it that has died?

K: The images have died. 'Me' is dead.

B: But is that a genuine death?

K: Ah, that is what I want to find out. Is it a verbal comprehension?

B: Or, more deeply, is there something that has to die? Something real. In other words if an organism dies something real has died. But when the self dies . . .

K: Ah, but I have accepted so far that the self has been an astonishingly real thing.

B: Yes.

K: Then you three come along and tell me that that image is fictitous. I understand that, and I am a little frightened that when that dies, when there is no image, there is an ending to something.

B: Yes, well what is it that ends?

K: Ah, quite. What is it that ends?

B: Is it something real that ends? You could say that an ending of an image is no ending at all—right?

K: At all . . .

B: If it is only an image that ends it is only an image of ending. What I am trying to say is that nothing much ends if it is only an image.

K: Yes. That is what I want to get at.

B: Is it? You know what I mean?

K: If it is merely an ending of an image . . .

S: . . . then that is nothing much.

B: It is like turning off the television. Is that what death is? Or is there something deeper that dies?

K: Oh, very much deeper.

B: Something deeper dies?

K: Yes.

S: How about the image-making process?

K: No, no. I would say it is not the end of the image which is death, but something much deeper.

B: But it is still not the death of the organism.

K: Still not the death of the organism, of course. The organism will more or less . . .

B: . . . go on, up to a point.

K: Up to a point, yes. There is disease, accident, old age. But death. The ending of the image is fairly simple, and fairly acceptable. But that is a very shallow pool.

B: Yes.

K: You have taken away the little water there is in the pool and there is nothing but mud left behind. That is nothing. So is there something much more?

S: That dies?

K: No. Not that dies, but to the meaning of death.

S: Is there something more than the image that dies, or does death have a meaning beyond the death of the image?

K: That is what we are asking.

S: Is there something about death that is bigger than the death of the image?

K: Obviously, it must be.

119

B: Will this include the death of the organism, this meaning?

K: The organism might go on, but eventually it comes to an end.

B: Yes, but if we were to see what death means as a whole, universally, then we would also see what the death of the organism means. But is there some meaning also in the death of the self-image? The same meaning?

K: That is only, I should say, a very small part.

B: That is very small.

K: That is a very, very small part.

B: But there might be a process or a structure beyond the self-image that might die, that creates the self-image.

K: Yes, that is thought.

B: That is thought. Now are you discussing the death of thought?

K: That again is only superficial.

B: That is very small.

K: Very small.

B: Is there something beyond thought in this that . . .?

K: That is what I want to get at.

S: We are trying to get at the meaning of death . . .

B: We are not quite there.

S: . . . which is beyond the death of the self, thought or the image.

K: No, just look: the image dies, that is fairly simple.

S: Right.

K: It is a very shallow affair. Then there is the ending of thought, which is dying to thought.

B: You said thought is deeper than the image but still not very deep.

K: Not very deep. Now is there something more?

B: In what sense "more"? Something more that exists? Or something more that has to die?

S: Is it something creative that happens?

K: No, no. We are going to find out.

120

B: But I mean your question is not clear when you say, "Is there something more?"

K: Death must have something enormously significant.

B: But are you saying that death has a meaning, a significance, for everything? For the whole of life?

K: For the whole of life.

B: It is not generally accepted, if we are thinking of the viewer, that death has that significance. As we live now death is . . .

K: . . . is at the end.

B: . . . is at the end and we try to forget about it.

K: Yes.

B: Try to make it unobtrusive.

K: But as you three have pointed out, my life has been in a turmoil, my life has been a constant conflict . . .

B: Right.

K: That has been my life. I have clung to the known and therefore death is the unknown, so I am afraid of it. And you come along and say, "Look, death is partly the ending of the image and the maker of the image, but death has much greater significance than merely this empty saucer."

B: Well, if you could make it more clear why it must have.

S: Why must it?

K: Is life just a shallow, empty pool? Empty mud at the end of it?

S: Why would you assume it is anything else?

K: I want to know.

B: But even if it is something else we have to ask why is it that death is the key to understanding.

K: Because it is the ending of everything. The end of reality and all my concepts, my images—the end of all the memories.

B: But that is in the ending of thought, right?

K: The ending of thought. It also means the ending of time.

B: Ending of time.

K: Time coming to a stop totally. There is no future in the sense of the past meeting the present and carrying on.

B: Psychologically speaking.

K: Yes, psychologically speaking, of course; we are speaking psychologically. Psychological ending to everything.

S: Right.

K: That's what death is.

B: And when your organism dies then everything ends for that organism.

K: Of course. When the organism dies it is finished. But wait a minute. If I don't end the image, the stream of image-making goes on.

B: It is not too clear where it goes on. In other people?

K: It manifests itself in other people. That is, I die; the organism dies and at the last minute I am still with the image that I have.

B: Yes, well then what happens to that?

K: That image has its continuity with the rest of the images, your image, my image.

S: Right.

K: Your image is not different from mine.

S: Right. We share that.

K: No, no. Not share it. It is not different. It may be a little more frail, or have a little more colour, but essentially my image is your image.

S: Right.

K: So there is this constant flow of image-making.

B: Well, where does it take place? In people?

K: It is there. It manifests itself in people.

B: You feel it is in some ways more general, more universal?

K: Yes, much more universal.

B: That is rather strange.

K: Eh?

B: I say it is rather strange to think of that.

K: Yes.

S: It is there. Like a river, it is there.

K: Yes, it is there.

S: And it manifests itself in streams.

B: In people.

S: Which we call people.

K: No, that stream is the maker of images and imagery.

B: In other words you are saying that the image does not originate only in one brain, but is in some sense universal?

K: Universal. Quite right.

B: You are not only saying that it is just the sum of all the brains; you are implying something more?

K: It is the effect of all the brains and it manifests itself in people as they are born.

B: Yes.

K: Now is that all? Let's say, yes. Does death bring about this sense of enormous, endless energy which has no beginning and no end? Life must have infinite depth.

B: Yes, and it is death which opens that out.

K: Death opens that up.

B: But we say it is more than the death of the image-making. You see, this is not clear. Is it something real which is blocking that from realizing itself?

K: Yes. It is blocking itself through images and the thought-maker.

S: The image-making and thought-making are blocking this greater . . .

K: Wait a minute. There are still other blocks, deeper blocks.

B: That is what I was trying to get at. That there are deeper blocks that are real.

K: That are real.

B: And they really have to die.

K: That is just it.

S: Would that be like this stream that you were talking about . . . .?

K: There is a stream of sorrow, isn't there?

B: Is sorrow deeper than the image?

K: Yes.

B: That is important.

K: It is.

S: You think so?

K: Don't you?

S: I do.

K: Be careful, sir, this is very serious.

S: That's right.

B: Would you say sorrow and suffering are the same, just different words?

K: Different words.

S: Deeper than this image-making is sorrow.

K: Isn't it? Man has lived with sorrow a million years.

B: Well, could we say a little more about sorrow. It is more than pain.

K: Much more than pain. Much more than loss. Much more than losing someone.

S: It is deeper than that.

K: Much deeper than that.

B: It goes beyond the image, beyond thought.

K: Of course. It goes beyond thought.

B: Beyond thought, and what we ordinarily call feeling.

K: Of course. Feeling, thought. Now can that end?

S: Before you go on—are you saying that the stream of sorrow is a different stream from the stream of image-making?

K: No, it is part of the stream.

S: Part of the same stream?

K: The same stream but much deeper.

B: Then are you saying that there is a very deep stream, and that image-making is on the surface of this stream?

K: That's all.

B: Right. The waves on the surface, right? Could you say we have understood the waves on the surface of this stream, which we call image-making?

K: Yes, that's right. Image-making.

B: And the disturbances in sorrow come out on the surface as image-making.

K: That's right.

S: So now we have got to go deep-sea diving!

K: You know, sir, there is universal sorrow.

B: Yes, but let's try to make it clear. It is not merely that there is the sum of all the sorrow of different people . . .

K: No, no. Could we put it this way? The waves on the river don't bring compassion or love—compassion, love, we have said, are synonymous, so we will keep to the word "compassion". The waves don't bring this. What will? Without compassion human beings are destroying themselves. So does compassion come with the ending of sorrow, which is not the sorrow created by thought?

B: In thought you have sorrow for the self—right?

K: Yes. Sorrow for the self.

B: Which is self-pity.

K: Self-pity.

B: And now you say there is another sorrow, a deeper sorrow.

K: There is a deeper sorrow.

B: Which is not merely the total sum but something universal.

K: That's right.

S: Can we spell that out? Go into it?

K: Don't you know it? I am just asking. Don't you know, aren't you aware of a much deeper sorrow than the sorrow of thought, of self-pity, the sorrow of the image?

S: Yes.

B: Is it sorrow for the fact that man is in this state which he can't get out of?

K: That is partly it. That means partly the sorrow of ignorance.

B: Yes. Man is ignorant and cannot get out of it.

K: Cannot get out of it. And the perception of that sorrow is compassion.

B: All right. Then the non-perception is sorrow?

K: Yes, yes, yes. Are we seeing the same thing?

S: No, I don't think so.

K: Say, for instance, you see me in ignorance.

B: Or I see the whole of mankind in ignorance.

K: Mankind in ignorance. Ignorant in the sense we are talking about—that is, the maker of the image . . .

B: Let's say that if my mind is really right, good, clear, that should have a deep effect on me.

S: What would have a deep effect on me?

B: To see this tremendous ignorance, this tremendous destruction.

K: We are getting at it. We are getting at it.

S: Right, right.

K: We are getting at it.

B: But then if I don't fully perceive, if I start to escape the perception of it, I am in it too.

K: Yes, in it too.

B: The feeling is that universal sorrow is still something I can feel, is that what you mean to say?

K: Yes.

B: Although I am not very perceptive as to what it means.

K: No, no. You can feel the sorrow of thought.

B: The sorrow of thought. But I can sense, or somehow be aware of the universal sorrow.

K: Yes.

B: Right.

S: You say universal sorrow is there whether you feel it . . .

K: You can feel it.

B: Feel it or sense it.

K: Sorrow of man living like this.

126

B: Is that the essence of it?

K: I am just moving into it. Let's go.

B: Is there more to it than that?

K: Much more to it.

B: Then perhaps we should try to bring that out.

K: I am trying to. You see me: I live the ordinary life, image, sorrow, fear, anxiety; I have the sorrow of self-pity. And you, who are "enlightened" (in quotes), look at me, and I say, "Aren't you full of sorrow for me?"—which is compassion.

B: I would say that is a kind of energy which is tremendously aroused because of this situation.

K: Yes.

B: But would you call it sorrow? Or compassion?

K: Compassion, which is the outcome of sorrow.

B: But have you felt sorrow first? I mean, does the enlightened person feel sorrow and then compassion?

K: No.

S: The other way?

K: No, no. Go very carefully. You see, sir, you are saying that one must have sorrow first to have compassion.

B: I am not. I am just exploring.

K: Yes, you are exploring. Through sorrow you come to compassion.

B: That is what you seem to be saying.

K: Which implies that I must go through all the horrors of mankind . . .

S: Right.

B: Well, let's say that the enlightened man sees this sorrow, sees this destruction, and he feels some tremendous energy—we will call it compassion.

K: Yes.

B: Now does he understand that the people are in sorrow . . .?

K: Of course.

127

B: . . . but he himself is not in sorrow.

K: That's right. That's right.

B: But he feels a tremendous energy to do something.

K: Yes. Tremendous energy of compassion.

S: Would you say then that the enlightened man perceives, or is aware of, the conflict, the awkwardness, the blundering, the loss of life, but that he is not aware of sorrow?

K: No, sir. Dr Shainberg just listen. Suppose you have been through all this—image, thought, the sorrow of thought, fears, anxieties, and you say, "I have understood all that". But you have very little left. You have energy, but it is a very shallow business. And is life as shallow as all that? Or has it an immense depth? Depth is the wrong word.

B: Well, yes, inwardness?

K: Inwardness, yes. And to find that out don't you have to die to everything known?

B: But how does this relate to sorrow at the same time?

K: I am coming to that. You might feel that I am ignorant, that I have my anxieties and fears. You are beyond it, you are on the other side of the stream as it were. Don't you have compassion for me?

S: Yes.

B: Yes.

K: Compassion. Is that the result of the ending of sorrow, universal sorrow?

B: Universal sorrow? You say the ending of sorrow. Now you are talking about the person who is in sorrow to begin with.

K: Yes.

B: And in him this universal sorrow ends? Is that what you are saying?

K: No. More than that.

B: More than that? Well, we have to go slowly because if you say the ending of universal sorrow, the thing that is puzzling is to say that it still exists, do you see?

K: Eh?

B: You say if the universal sorrow ends then it has all gone.

K: Ah, it is still there.

B: Still there. There is a certain puzzle in language.

K: Yes, yes.

B: So in some sense the universal sorrow ends, but in another sense it persists.

K: Yes, that is right.

B: Could we say that if you have an insight into the essence of sorrow, universal sorrow, then sorrow ends in that insight? Is that what you mean?

K: Yes, that's right.

B: Although . . .

K: Although it still goes on.

S: I have got a deeper question. The question is . . .

K: I don't think you have understood.

S: Oh, I think I have understood that one, but my question comes before, which is that the image-making has died—right? That is, the waves. Now I come into the sorrow.

K: You have lost the sorrow of thought.

S: Right. The sorrow of thought has gone but there is a deeper sorrow.

K: Is there? Or are you assuming there is a deeper sorrow?

S: I am trying to see what you are saying.

K: No, no. I am saying: Is there compassion which is not related to thought? Or is that compassion born of sorrow?

S: Born of sorrow?

K: Born in the sense that when the sorrow ends there is compassion.

S: OK. That makes it a little clearer. When the sorrow of thought . . .

K: Not personal sorrow.

S: No. When the sorrow . . .

K: Not the sorrow of thought.

B: Not the sorrow of thought, something deeper.

S: Something deeper. When that sorrow ends then there is a birth of compassion.

B: Of compassion, of energy.

K: Now is there not a deeper sorrow than the sorrow of thought?

S: There is. As you were saying, there is sorrow for ignorance which is deeper than thought—the sorrow for the universal calamity of mankind trapped in this sorrow, the sorrow for a continual repetition of wars and poverty and people mistreating each other, that's a deeper sorrow.

K: I understand all that.

S: That is deeper than the sorrow of thought.

K: Can we ask this question: What is compassion? Which is love. We are using that one word to cover a wide field. What is compassion? Can a man who is in sorrow, in thought, in the image—can he have that? He cannot. Actually he cannot—right?

B: Yes.

K: Now when does that compassion come into being? Without that life has no meaning. You have left me without that. All you have taken away from me is superficial sorrow, thought and image-making. And I feel there is something much more.

B: Just doing that leaves something empty.

K: Yes.

B: Meaningless.

K: There is something much greater than this shallow little business.

B: When we have thought which produces sorrow, self-pity, and when we also have the realization of the sorrow of mankind, could you say that the energy which is deeper is in some ways being . . .?

K: . . . moved.

B: . . . moved. Well, first of all in this sorrow this energy is . . .

K: . . . caught.

B: . . . is caught up in whirlpools or something. It is deeper than thought but there is some sort of very deep disturbance of the energy.

130

K: Quite right.

B: Which we call deep sorrow.

K: Deep sorrow.

B: Ultimately its origin is the blockage in thought, isn't it?

K: Yes, that is deep sorrow of mankind. For centuries upon centuries it has been like that—you know, like a vast reservoir of sorrow.

B: It is sort of moving around in some way that is disorderly.

K: Yes.

B: And preventing clarity. I mean perpetuating ignorance.

K: Yes, perpetuating ignorance, right.

B: Because if it were not for that then man's natural capacity to learn would solve all these problems.

K: That's right.

S: Right, right.

K: Unless you three give me, or help me, or show me, an insight into something much greater, I say, "Yes, this is very nice", and off I go—you follow? What we are trying to do, as far as I can see, is to penetrate into something beyond death.

B: Beyond death?

K: Death we say is not only the ending of the organism, but the ending of the content of the consciousness—consciousness as we know it now.

B: Is it also the ending of sorrow?

K: The ending of sorrow of the superficial kind. That is clear.

B: Yes.

K: And a man who has gone through all that says, "That isn't good enough. You haven't given me the flower, the perfume. You have just given me the ashes of it." And now we three are trying to find out that which is beyond the ashes.

S: Right.

B: There is that which is beyond death?

K: Ah, absolutely.

B: Would you say that is eternal, or . . .

K: I don't want to use that word.

B: I mean is it in some sense beyond time?

K: Beyond time.

B: Therefore eternal is not the best word.

K: There is something beyond the superficial death, a movement that has no beginning and no ending.

B: But it is a movement?

K: It is a movement. Movement, not in time.

S: What is the difference between a movement in time, and a movement out of time?

K: Sir, that which is constantly renewing, constantly—new isn't the word—constantly fresh, endlessly flowering, that is timeless. But this word flowering implies time.

B: I think we can see the point.

S: I think we get that, the feel of renewal in creation, and coming and going without transition, without duration, without linearity.

K: Let me come back to it in a different way. Being a fairly intelligent man, having read various books, tried various meditations, at one glance I have an insight into all that, at one glance—which is the end of image-making. It is finished. I won't touch it. Then a meditation must take place to delve, to have an insight, into something which the mind has never touched before.

B: But even if you do touch, it doesn't mean that the next time it will be known.

K: Ah, it can never be known in a sense.

B: It can never be known. It's always new in some sense.

K: Yes, it is always new. It is not a memory stored up, altered, changed, and called new. It has never been old. I don't know if I can put it that way.

B: Yes. I think I understand that. But could you say it is like a mind that has never known sorrow?

K: Yes.

B: It might seem puzzling at first. You move out of this state which has known sorrow into a state which has not known sorrow.

K: Quite right, sir.

B: In other words there is no you.

K: That's right, that's right.

S: Can we say it in this way too—that it is an action which is moving where there is no you?

K: You see when you use the word "action", it means not in the future, nor in the past; action is doing.

S: Yes.

K: And most of our actions are the result of the past, or according to a future ideal. That's not action, that is just conformity.

S: Right. I am talking about a different kind of action.

K: To penetrate into this, the mind must be completely silent. Otherwise you are projecting something into it.

S: Right. It is not projecting into anything.

K: Absolute silence. And that silence is not the product of control—wished for, premeditated, predetermined.

S: Right.

K: Therefore that silence is not brought about through will.

S: Right.

K: Now in that silence there is this sense of something beyond all time, all death, all thought—you follow? Nothing. Not a thing, you understand, nothing. And therefore empty and therefore tremendous energy.

B: Is this also the source of compassion?

K: That's it.

S: What do you mean by source?

B: Well, in this energy is compassion . . .

K: Yes, that is right.

S: In this energy is . . .

K: This energy is.

B: Compassion.

S: That's different.

K: Of course.

S: This energy is compassion. You see that is different from saying the source.

K: You see, beyond that there is something more.

S: Beyond that?

K: Of course.

B: Why do you say of course? What could it be that is more?

K: Sir, let us put it, approach it, differently. Everything thought has created is not sacred, is not holy.

B: Because it is fragmented.

K: It is fragmented. We know that putting up an image and worshipping it is a creation of thought.

S: That's right.

K: Made by the hand, or by the mind, it is still an image. So in that there is nothing sacred. Because, as Dr Bohm pointed out, thought is fragmented, limited, finite; it is the product of memory and so on.

B: Is the sacred, therefore, that which is without limit?

K: That's it. There is something beyond compassion.

B: Beyond compassion.

K: Which is sacred.

B: Is it beyond movement?

K: Sacred. You can't say movement, or non-movement. A living thing—you can only examine a dead thing.

S: Right.

K: A living thing you can't examine. What we are trying to do is to examine that living thing which we call sacred, which is beyond compassion.

B: What is our relation to the sacred then?

K: To the man who is ignorant there is no relationship—right? Which is true. To the man who is free of the image and the image-maker, it has no meaning yet—right? It has meaning only when he goes beyond everything, dies to everything. Dying means never for a single second accumulating anything psychologically.

S: But he asked the question: What is the relationship to the sacred? Is there ever a relationship to the sacred?

134

K: No, no. He is asking what is the relationship between that which is sacred, holy, and reality.

B: Well, that is implicit anyway. I mean that is implied.

K: Of course. We have talked about this question some time ago. Reality, which is the product of thought, has no relationship to that because thought is an empty little affair.

S: Right.

K: Relationship comes through insight, intelligence and compassion.

S: What is intelligence, I suppose we are asking. I mean, how does intelligence act?

K: Wait, wait. You have had an insight into the image. You have had an insight into the movement of thought—the movement of thought which is self-pity, which creates sorrow. You have had a real insight into that. Haven't you? It is not a verbal agreement or disagreement or a logical conclusion. You have had a real insight into that, into the waves of the river.

S: Right.

K: Now isn't that insight intelligence?

S: Right.

K: Which is not the intelligence of a clever man, we are not talking about that. Now work with that intelligence, which is not yours or mine, not Dr Shainberg's or Dr Bohm's, or somebody's. That insight is universal intelligence, global or cosmic intelligence. Now move further into it. Have an insight into sorrow, which is not the sorrow of thought. Then out of that insight compassion. Now have insight into compassion. Is compassion the end of all life? End of all death? It seems so because the mind throws out all the burdens which man has imposed upon himself—right? So you have that tremendous feeling, that tremendous thing inside. Now that compassion, delve into it. And there is something sacred, untouched by man—in the sense of being untouched by his mind, by his cravings, by his demands, by his prayers, by his everlasting chicanery. And that may be the origin of everything, which man has misused—you follow?

B: If you say it is the origin of all matter, all nature . . .

K: Everything, all matter, all nature.

B: All of mankind.

K: Yes. That's right, sir. So at the end of these dialogues, what have you, what has the viewer got, what has he captured?

S: What would we hope he has got? Would you say what we hope he has captured, or what he has actually captured?

K: What he has actually, not hope. What has he actually captured? Has his bowl filled?

S: Filled with the sacred.

K: Or does he say, "Well I have got a lot of ashes left, very kind of you, but I can get that anywhere". Any logical, rational, human being would say, "They are discussing my part in all this and I am left with nothing".

S: What has he got?

K: He has come to you—I have come to you three wanting to find out, wanting to transform my life, because I feel that is absolutely necessary, not just to get rid of my ambitions and all the silly stuff mankind has collected—I have emptied myself of all that—the I has died to all that. Now have I got anything out of all this? Have you given me the perfume of that thing?

S: Can I give you the perfume?

K: Or share it with me.

S: Has the viewer shared with us the experience we have had being together?

K: Have you two shared this thing with this man?

S: Have we shared this with this man?

K: If not, then what? A clever discussion—oh, we are fed up with that. You can only share when you are really hungry—burning with hunger. Otherwise you share words. So I have come to the point, we have come to the point, when we see that life has an extraordinary meaning.

B: Yes, it has a meaning far beyond what we usually think.

K: Yes, that is so shallow and empty.

B: So would you say this sacred is also life?

K: Yes, that's what I was getting at. Life is sacred.

B: And the sacred is life.

S: Have we shared that?

K: Have you shared that? So we mustn't misuse life. We mustn't waste it because our life is so short.

B: You feel that each of our lives has a part to play in this sacred which you talked about? It is a part of the whole, and to use it rightly has a tremendous significance?

K: Yes, quite right. But to accept it as a theory is as good as any other theory.

S: Right. But somehow I feel troubled. Have we shared it? That burns, that question burns. Have we shared the sacred?

K: Which really means that all these discussions, dialogues, have been a process of meditation. Not a clever argument, but a real penetrating meditation which brings insight into everything that is being said.

B: Well, I should say we have been doing that.

K: I think we have been doing that.

S: And have we shared that?

B: With whom?

S: With the viewer?

K: Ah, are you considering the viewer? Or is there no viewer at all? Are you speaking to the viewer, or only to that thing in which the viewer, you and I, and everything is? You understand what I am saying?

S: You said we have been in a meditation, and I say we have been in a meditation—but how far have we shared our meditation?

K: No. I mean has it been a meditation?

S: Yes.

K: Meditation is not just argument.

S: No, we have shared in that.

K: Seeing the truth of every statement.

S: Right.

K: Or the falseness of every statement. Or seeing in the false the truth.

137

S: Right. Then being aware of the false in each of us as it comes out and is clarified.

K: Seeing it all, and therefore we are in a state of meditation. And whatever we say must then lead to that ultimate thing. Then you are not sharing.

S: Where are you?

K: There is no sharing. It is only that.

S: The act of meditation is that.

K: There is only that.

PART II

The substance of the public talks given in Ojai, California; Saanen, Switzerland; and Brockwood Park, England, during 1977.

I

Meditation is the emptying of the content of consciousness

Meditation is one of the most important things in life; not how to meditate; not meditation according to a system; not the practice of meditation; but rather that which meditation is. If one can find out, very deeply, the significance, the necessity and the importance of it for oneself, then one puts aside all systems, methods, gurus, together with all the peculiar things that are involved in the Eastern type of meditation.

It is very important to uncover for oneself what one actually is; not according to the theories and the assertions and experiences of psychologists, philosophers and the gurus, but rather by investigating the whole nature and movement of oneself; by seeing what one actually is.

One does not seem to be able to understand how extraordinarily important it is to see what one is, actually, as though one is looking at oneself in a mirror, psychologically; thereby bringing about a transformation in the very structure of oneself. When one fundamentally, deeply, brings about such a transformation, or mutation, then that mutation affects the whole consciousness of man. This is an absolute fact, a reality. To bring about a fundamental transformation becomes very important, if one is at all serious, if one is concerned with the world as it is, with all its appalling misery, confusion and uncertainty, with all the divisions of religions and nationalities, with their wars, with their accumulation of armaments, spending enormous sums to prepare for war, to kill people, in the name of nationality and so on and so on.

To see what one actually is, it is vital that there be freedom, freedom from the whole content of one's consciousness; the content of consciousness being all the things put together by thought. Freedom from the content of one's consciousness, from one's angers and brutalities, from one's vanities and arrogance, from all the things that one is caught up in, is meditation. The very seeing of what one is, is the beginning of the transformation. Meditation implies the ending of all strife, of all conflict, inwardly and therefore outwardly. Actually, there is no inward or outward, it is like the sea, there is the ebb and flow.

In uncovering what one actually is, one asks: Is the observer, oneself, different from that which one observes—psychologically that is. I am angry, I am greedy, I am violent; is that I different from the thing observed, which is anger, greed, violence? Is one different? Obviously not. When I am angry there is no I that is angry, there is only anger. So anger is me; the observer is the observed. The division is eliminated altogether. The observer is the observed and therefore conflict ends.

Part of meditation is to eliminate totally all conflict, inwardly and therefore outwardly. To eliminate conflict one has to understand this basic principle; the observer is not different from the observed, psychologically. When there is anger, there is no I, but a second later thought creates the I and says: "I have been angry" and brings in the idea that I should not be angry. So there is anger and then the I who should not be angry; the division brings conflict. When there is no division between the observer and the observed, and therefore only the thing that is, which is anger, then what takes place? Does anger go on? Or is there a total ending of anger? When anger occurs and there is no observer, no division, it blossoms and then ends—like a flower, it blooms, withers and dies away. But as long as one is fighting it, as long as one is resisting it, or rationalizing it, one is giving life to it. When the observer is the observed, then anger blossoms, grows and naturally dies—therefore there is no psychological conflict in it.

One lives by action; action according to a motive, according to an ideal, according to a pattern, or habitual and traditional action, all without any investigation. A mind that is in meditation must find out what action is. One of the major problems in one's life is conflict and from conflict all kinds of neurotic activities arise. To end conflict and therefore to end neurotic action, is very important, so that one has a sane mind, a mind that is healthy, a mind that is not neurotically caught in beliefs and fears and so on.

How does one act, according to what principle, according to what quality or state of mind does one act? Generally one acts from memory, the memory which is set in a pattern, which has become habit, routine. One acts according to that which is remembered as pleasant; or one acts according to an ideal one has determined to carry out in daily life; or one has an ambition which one tries to fulfil. There are various types of action and each of them is incomplete, fragmented; none is holistic—"I'm a business man and I come home and I love my children, but when I'm at business, there, I do not love anybody, I want profit, etc. etc.; I may be a scholar, a painter, but my life—though I am an excellent painter—is shoddy, I'm vicious, greedy, wanting money, position, recognition, fame."

One's actions are divided, fragmentary and when there is fragmentary action it must inevitably bring conflict, psychologically. Is there an action which is without conflict in which there are no regrets, no failures, no sense of frustration; is there an action which is whole, harmonious, complete, an action not in a particular field contrary to another field? One has to see what one is actually doing, how one is actually living a contradictory life, acting contradictorily and therefore in conflict. One must become aware of it. And if one is completely aware, then what takes place?

Suppose I live in contradictory actions and you tell me, "Be aware of it". What do you mean by being aware of it?—I ask. Awareness is not possible when you choose, when you say: "I like that particular action, I would like to keep that; please help me to avoid all other action." That is not awareness; that is choosing a particular action which appears most satisfactory, most comforting, most gratifying, rewarding and so on. Where there is choice there is no complete awareness. If one is completely aware, there is no problem. There is then an action which is continuous, without any break and therefore holistic. It is to have a mind that is sane, which implies not being committed to any particular form of belief, dogma, or ideal, nothing. It is to have a mind able to think clearly, directly, objectively. In the process of meditation one comes to find that action.

To find out what meditation is, all previous knowledge of what meditation is thought to be blocks the exploration. Freedom from psychological authority is absolutely necessary. What is necessary in the investigation? Is it concentration; is it attention or is it awareness? When one concentrates, one's whole energy is focused on something particular, one resists and puts aside all interfering thoughts. In concentration one is resisting. But to be aware of one's thought there is no concentration; one does not choose in awareness which thought one would like; one is just aware. From that awareness comes attention. In attention there is no centre from which one is attending. This is really important to understand, it is the essence of meditation. In concentration there is a centre from which one is concentrating, on a picture or on an idea or on some image, etc.; one is exercising energy in concentration, in resisting, building a wall, so that no other thought comes in and there must be conflict. To totally eliminate that conflict become choicelessly aware of thought; then there is no contradiction, no resistance about any thought. From that arises awareness; awareness of all the movement of one's thought. Out of that awareness comes attention. When one is attending to something, really deeply, there is no centre; there is no me.

In attention—if one has gone that far—one is free from all the travails of thought, its fears, agonies and despairs; that is the foundation. The content of one's consciousness is being emptied; it is being freed. Meditation is the emptying of the content of consciousness. That is the meaning and the depth of meditation, the emptying of all the content—thought coming to an end.

Meditation is the attention in which there is no registration. Normally the brain is registering almost everything, the noise, the words which are being used—it is registering like a tape. Now is it possible for the brain not to register except that which is absolutely necessary? Why should I register an insult? Why? Why should I register flattery? It is unnecessary. Why should I register any hurts? Unnecessary. Therefore, register only that which is necessary in order to operate in daily life—as a technician, a writer and so on—but psychologically, do not register anything. In meditation there is no registration psychologically, no registration except the practical facts of living, going to the office, working in a factory and so on—nothing else. Out of that comes complete silence, because thought has come to an end—except to function only where it is absolutely necessary. Time has come to an end and there is a totally different kind of movement, in silence.

Religion then has a totally different meaning, whereas before it was a matter of thought. Thought made the various religions and therefore each religion is fragmented and in each fragment there are multiple subdivisions. All that is called religion, including the

144

beliefs, the hopes, the fears and the desire to be secure in another world and so on, is the result of thought. It is not religion, it is merely the movement of thought, in fear, in hope, in trying to find security—a material process.

Then what is religion? It is the investigation, with all one's attention, with the summation of all one's energy, to find that which is sacred, to come upon that which is holy. That can only take place when there is freedom from the noise of thought—the ending of thought and time, psychologically, inwardly—but not the ending of knowledge in the world where you have to function with knowledge. That which is holy, that which is sacred, which is truth, can only be when there is complete silence, when the brain itself has put thought in its right place. Out of that immense silence there is that which is sacred.

Silence demands space, space in the whole structure of consciousness. There is no space in the structure of one's consciousness as it is, because it is crowded with fears—crowded, chattering, chattering. When there is silence, there is immense, timeless space; then only is there a possibility of coming upon that which is the eternal, sacred.

II

The ending of conflict is the
gathering of supreme energy which
is a form of intelligence

There is the theory of old, that god, divinity, descends on man and helps him to grow, to evolve and to live nobly. That is the old tradition of the countries in the East and also in a different way, in the West. In belief in such theories there is great comfort; a feeling that one is at least secure in something; that there is somebody that is looking after you and the world. That is a very old theory and it has no meaning whatsoever. That theory and teaching gives some kind of hope in a Utopia in the future as made by the present; a hope arising from the limits of what one is now. Unless there is a radical transformation, such a future is the modified continuity of "what is".

One realizes that there is no security whatsoever in the things that thought has put together if one has gone into it sufficiently intelligently, rationally and sanely to find out; one sees that there is really no structure, either in the future, or in the past, or in the present, philosophical, religious, or ideological, which can give any kind of security whatsoever.

One accepts very easily the path that is the most satisfying, the most convenient, the most pleasurable. It is very easy to move into that groove. And authority dictates, lays down, in a religious or a psychological system, a method by which, or through which, you are told you will find security. But if one sees that there is no security in any such authority, then one can find out whether it is possible to live without any guidance, without any control, without any effort psychologically. So, one is going to investigate, to see, whether the mind can be free to find the truth of this matter, so that one will never, under any circumstance, conform to any pattern of authority, psychologically.

When one is conforming to a pattern, religious, psychological, or the pattern which one has set for oneself, there is always a contradiction between what one actually is and the pattern. There is always a conflict and this conflict is endless. If one has finished with one pattern one goes to another. One is educated to live in this field of conflict because of these ideals, patterns, conclusions, beliefs and so on. Conforming to a pattern one is never free; one does not know what compassion is and one is always battling and therefore giving importance to oneself; the self becomes extraordinarily important with the idea of self-improvement.

So, is it possible to live without a pattern? Now, how is one, as a human being, the total representative of all mankind, how is one going to find out the truth of this matter? Because if one's consciousness is changed radically, profoundly—no, revolutionized rather than changed—then one affects the consciousness of the whole of mankind.

How is one going to go into this problem; with what capacity does one investigate? To investigate there must be freedom from motive. If one wants to investigate the question of authority, one's background says: I must obey, I must follow; and in the process one's background is always projecting, is always distorting one's investigation. Can one be free of one's background so that it does not interfere in any way with one's investigation? One's urgency to find the truth, one's immediacy, one's demand, puts the background in abeyance; one's intensity to find out is so strong that the background ceases to interfere. Although the background, one's education, one's conditioning, is so strong—it has accumulated for centuries; consciously one cannot fight it, one cannot push it aside; one cannot battle with it and one sees that to fight the background only intensifies the background—yet one's very intensity to find out the truth of authority puts that background much further away; it is no longer impinging on one's mind.

One needs to have tremendous energy to find out the truth of this matter. Mostly, this energy is dissipated in the conflict between "what is" and "what should be". One sees that "what should be" is an escape from, or an avoidance of, the fact of "what is". Or thought, incapable of meeting "what is", projects "what should be" and uses that as a lever to try to remove "what is". So is it possible to look at, to observe, "what is", without any motive to change or to transform it, or to make it conform to a particular pattern that you or another has established—whatever may happen at the end of it? If one does, the background fades away. If one is very intense to understand, one forgets oneself, forgets one is a Hindu, a Christian, a Buddhist, one forgets all one's background; therefore the whole thing disappears, the background, the motive, everything, because there is the present necessity and the urgency to find out.

The intensity that is necessary can only come into being when there is no cause and no effect and therefore no reaction. It implies that one must be completely alone in one's investigation. Aloneness does not mean isolation, it does not mean one is withdrawn and has built a wall around oneself. Alone means that one is all one. Then one is a total human being representing all humanity, one's consciousness has undergone a change through perception, which is the awakening of intelligence. That intelligence finishes forever with psychological authority; it profoundly affects one's consciousness.

Is it possible to live a life without any pattern, without any goal, without any idea of the future, a life without conflict? It is only possible when one lives completely with "what is". With "what is" means with that which is actually taking place. Live with it; do not try to transform it, do not try to go beyond it, do not try to control it, do not try to escape from it, just look at it, live with it. If you are envious, or greedy, jealous, or you have problems, sex, fear, whatever they are, live with them without any movement of thought that wants to move away from them. Which means what? One is not wasting one's energy in control, in suppression, in conflict, in resistance, in escape. All that energy was being wasted; now one has gathered it up. Because one sees the absurdity of it, the falseness of it, the unreality of it, one has now the energy to live with "what is"; one has that energy to observe without any movement of thought. It is the thought that has created jealousy and thought that says: "I must run away from it, I must escape from it, I must suppress it." If one sees that falseness of escape, resistance, suppression, then that energy which has gone into escape, resistance and suppression is gathered to observe. Then what takes place?

One is not escaping, not resisting and then one is envious, the envy being the result of the movement of thought. The envy arises from comparison, measurement—I have not, you have. And thought, because it has been educated to run away, runs away from this thing. Now because one sees the falseness of it one stops and one has the energy to observe this envy. That very word "envy" is its own condemnation. When one says "I am envious," there is already a sense of pushing it away. So, one must be free of the influence of the word to observe. And this demands tremendous alertness, tremendous watchfulness, awareness, so as not to escape and so as to see that the word envy has created the feeling; for without the word, is there the feeling? If there is no word and therefore no movement of thought, then is there envy?

The word has created the feeling because the word is associated with the feeling, it is dictating the feeling. Can one observe without the word? Now, words are the movement of thought used to communicate—communicate with oneself, or with another—when there are no words there is no communication between the fact and the observer. Therefore the movement of thought as envy has come to an end; come to an end completely, not temporarily—one can look at a beautiful car and observe the beauty of its lines and that is the end of it.

To live with "what is" completely, implies no conflict whatsoever. Therefore there is no future as transforming it into something else. The very ending of it is the gathering of supreme energy which is a form of intelligence.

III

Out of negation comes the
positive called love

Throughout the world human beings are always seeking security, both physiological and psychological. Physical security is denied when psychological security—which does not really exist—is sought in various forms of illusion and in divisive beliefs, dogmas, religious sanctions and so on. Where there are these psychological divisions, there must inevitably be physiological division with all its conflicts, wars and the suffering and the tragedy and the inhumanity of man to man. Wherever one goes in the world, it does not matter whether it is in India, Europe, Russia, China or America, human beings, psychologically, are more or less the same; they suffer, they are anxious, uncertain, confused, often in great pain, ambitious, fighting each other everlastingly.

Basically, psychologically, as all human beings are the same one can with reason say that the world is oneself and one is the world. That is an absolute fact, as one can see when one goes into it very deeply. And the content of human consciousness is the whole movement of thought and the desire for power, position, security and the pursuit of pleasure in which there is fear. Fear and pleasure are the two sides of the same coin. Without understanding the whole stucture and nature of pleasure, based on desire, one will never understand and live a life in which there is love.

Fear and the pursuit of pleasure are part of consciousness. But is love also a part of consciousness? When there is fear, is there love? When there is the mere pursuit of pleasure, is there love? Is love pleasure and desire, or has it nothing whatsoever to do with pleasure and desire?

One's brain, through the constant habit of seeking security has become mechanical; mechanical in the sense of following certain definite patterns, repeating these patterns over and over again in the routine of daily life. There is the repetition of pleasure and the burden of fear and the inability to resolve it. So, gradually, the brain, or part of the brain, has become mechanical, repetitive, biologically as well as psychologically; one is caught in certain patterns of belief, dogma, ideology—the American ideology, the Russian ideology, the ideology of India and so on. There is the direction, the pursuit, and the mind and the brain deteriorate.

However pleasant, the life one lives is a life that is repetitive; however desirable, however complex, it is a repetitive life—the same belief from childhood to death, the same rituals, whether it is church or temple, there is the tradition of it, over and over again. There is the repetition of pleasure, sexual pleasure or the pleasure of achievement, the pleasure of possession, the pleasure of attachment, all these cause the brain to deteriorate because they are repetitive. So long as there is the pursuit of pleasure as a repetitive process and the burden of fear which it brings and which man has not resolved—he has run away from it, escaped from it, rationalized it, but still it remains—the brain deteriorates.

What is love? Is it pleasure—pleasure in the repetitive sexual act, which is generally called love? The love of one's neighbour, the love of one's wife, in which there is great pleasure, possession and comfort, based on desire—is that love? Where there is possessive attachment to another, there must be jealousy, there must be fear and antagonism. These are obvious facts—nothing extraordinary or ideological—they are facts, "what is". So is attachment love? And what is the basis of attachment? Why is one attached to something, to property, to an idea, to an ideology, to a person, to a symbol, to a concept which is called God? If one does not fully understand the significance of attachment, then one will never be able to find the truth of love. Is not the basis of attachment the fear of being alone, the fear of being isolated, the emptiness, the sense of insufficiency in oneself?

We are attached to people, to ideas, to symbols, or to concepts, because in them we think there is security. Is there security in any relationship? Is there security—which is really the essence of attachment—in one's wife, or husband? And if one seeks security in the wife or the husband and so on, then what takes place? One possesses, legally or not legally. And where there is possession there must be fear of losing—therefore jealousy, hatred, divorce and all the rest of it.

Is love attachment? Can there be love when there is attachment; with all the implications of that word which include fear, jealousy, guilt, irritation leading to hatred—all that is implied when one uses the word "attachment"? Where there is attachment can there be love? These are factual, not theoretical, questions. One is dealing with daily life, not with some extraordinary life. One can only go very deeply and very far if one begins very near, which is oneself. If one does not understand oneself one cannot move far. One is delving into problems which are tremendously important in one's daily life.

Although one has to go into this question logically, rationally, sanely, one has to go beyond it; because logic is not love, reason is not love. The desire to be loved and to love is not love. Out of the negation of what is not love, every moment of one's life, out of the putting aside of what is not love, comes the positive thing called love.

Thought is fragmentary, limited; thought cannot solve the problem of what love is and thought cannot cultivate love. When one makes an abstraction in thought, one moves away from "what is". That movement of abstraction becomes a condition according to which one lives, therefore one no longer lives according to facts. This is what one has done all one's life; but one will never know what love is through abstraction, will not know the enormous beauty, depth and significance of love.

Why does man put up with this suffering? Why worship suffering, which the Christians do, apparently? What is the meaning of suffering? What is it that suffers? When one says "I suffer," who is it that suffers? What is the centre that says "I am in an agony of jealousy, of fear, of loss"? What is that centre, that "essence", of a human being who says "I suffer"? Is it the movement of thought, as time, which creates the centre? How does that I come into being, which, having come into being says, "I suffer, I am anxious, I am frightened, I am jealous, I am lonely". That I is never stationary, it is always moving: "I desire this, I desire that and then I desire something else", it is in constant movement. That movement is time, that movement is thought.

There is a concept in the Asiatic world that the I is something which is beyond time; and further, the concept that there is a higher I still. In the Western world the I has never been thoroughly examined. Qualities have been attributed to it, Freud and Jung and other psychologists have given attributes to it but have never gone into this question of the nature and the structure of the I which says "I suffer".

The I, as one observes, says "I must have that", a few days later it wants something else. There is the constant movement of desire; the constant movement of pleasure; the constant movement of what one wants to be and so on. This movement is thought as psychological time. The I who says "I suffer" is put together by thought. Thought says, "I am John, I am this, I am that". Thought identifies itself with the name and with the form and is the I in all the content of consciousness; it is the essence of fear, hurt, despair, anxiety, guilt, the pursuit of pleasure, the sense of loneliness, all the content of consciousness. When one says "I suffer", it is the image that thought has built about itself, the form, the name, that is in sorrow.

The more intense the challenge is, the greater is the energy demanded to meet it. Sorrow is this challenge. To that challenge one has to respond. But if one responds to it by escaping from it, by seeking comfort from it, then one is dissipating the energy that one needs to meet this thing.

There is no escape—there is no escape because if one tries to escape, sorrow is always there, like one's shadow, like one's face, it is always with one—so remain with it, without any movement of thought. If one runs away from it, one has not solved it; but if one remains with it, not identifying oneself with it—because one is that suffering—then all your energy is present to meet this extraordinary thing that happens. Out of that suffering comes passion.

There is a solution, there is an ending to sorrow—as there is an ending to fear—completely. Then only is there a possibility to know what love is. One thinks that one will learn something from suffering, that there is a lesson to be learnt from suffering. But when one observes suffering in oneself, not escaping from it, but remaining with it totally, completely, without any movement of thought, without any alleviation, comfort, but just completely holding to it, then one will see a strange psychological transformation take place.

Love is passion, which is compassion. Without that passion and compassion, with its intelligence, one acts in a very limited sense; all one's actions are limited. Where there is compassion that action is total, complete, irrevocable.

153

IV

Death—a great act of purgation

Death is something not only mysterious but a great act of purgation. That which continues in a repetitive pattern is degeneration. The pattern may vary according to country, according to climate, according to circumstance, but it is a pattern. Moving in any pattern brings about a continuity and that continuity is part of the degenerating process of man. When there is an ending of continuity, something new can take place. One can understand it instantly if one has understood the whole movement of thought, of fear, hate, love—then one can grasp the significance, instantly, of what death is.

What is death? When one asks that question, thought has many answers. Thought says: "I do not want to go into all the miserable explanations of death." Every human being has an answer to it, according to his conditioning, according to his desire, his hope. Thought always has an answer. The answer will invariably be intellectual, verbally put together by thought. But one is examining, without having an answer, something totally unknown, totally mysterious—death is a tremendous thing.

One realizes that the organism, the body, dies and the brain—having in life been misused in various forms of self-indulgence, contradiction, effort, constant struggle, wearing itself out mechanically, for it is a mechanism—also dies. The brain is the repository of memory; memory as experience, as knowledge. From that experience and knowledge, stored up in the cells of the brain, as memory, thought arises. When the organism comes to an end, the brain also comes to an end, and so thought comes to an end. Thought is a material process—thought is nothing spiritual—it is a material process based on memory held in the cells of the brain; when the organism dies, thought dies. Thought creates the whole structure of the me—the me that wants this, the me that does not want that, the me that is fearful, anxious, despairing, longing, lonely—fearful of dying. And thought says: "What is the value, what is the significance of life for a human being who has struggled, experienced, acquired, lived in such an ugly, stupid, miserable way and then for it to end?" So, thought then says: "No, this is not the end, there is another world." But that other world is still merely the movement of thought.

One asks what happens after death. Now ask quite a different question: What is before death?—not what is after death. What is before death, which is one's life. What is one's life? Go to school, to college, university, get a job, man and woman live together, he goes off to the office for 50 years, she goes off earning more money, they have children, pain, anxiety, each fighting. Living such a miserable life one wants to know what is after death—about which volumes have been written, all produced by thought, all saying, "Believe". So, if one puts all that aside, literally, actually, puts it all aside, then what is one faced with?—the actual fact that oneself who is put together by thought, comes to an end—all one's anxieties, all one's longings come to an end. When one is living, as one is living now, with vigour, with energy, with all the travail of life, can one live meeting death now? I am living in all vigour, energy and capacity, and death means an ending to that living. Now, can I live with death all the time? That is: I am attached to you; end that attachment, which is death—is it not? One is greedy and when one dies, one cannot carry greed with one; so end the greed, not in a week's time, or ten days' time—end it, now. So one is living a life full of vigour, energy, capacity, observation, seeing the beauty of the earth and also the ending of that instantly, which is death. So to live before death is to live with death; which means that one is living in a timeless world. One is living a life in which everything that one acquires is constantly ending, so that there is always a tremendous movement, one is not fixed in a certain place. This is not a concept. When one invites death, which means the ending of everything that one holds, dying to it, each day, each minute, then one will find—not "one" there is then no oneself finding it, because one has gone—then there is that state of a timeless dimension in which the movement we know as time, is not. It means the emptying of the content of one's consciousness so that there is no time; time comes to an end, which is death.

V

Action which is skilful and which does not perpetuate the self

We have become very skilful in dealing with our daily life; skilful, in the sense of being clever in applying a great deal of knowledge which we have acquired through education and through experience. We act skilfully, either in a factory, or in a business and so on. That skill becomes, through repetitive action, routine. Skill, when it is highly developed—as it should be—leads to self importance and self aggrandizement. Skill has brought us to our present state, not only technologically but in our relationships, in the way we deal with each other—not clearly, not with compassion, but with skill. Is there an action, in our daily life, which is skilful yet which does not perpetuate the self, the me, which does not give importance to oneself and to one's self-centred existence? Is it possible to act skilfully without strengthening the self? To answer that one has to enquire into what clarity is; when there is clarity there is action which is skilful and which does not perpetuate the self.

Clarity exists only when there is freedom to observe. One is only capable of observing, looking, watching, when there is complete and total freedom; otherwise there is always distortion in the observation. Is it possible to be free of all the distorting factors in one's outlook? When one observes oneself, or another, or society, the environment, the whole cultural, political and religious movements that are going on in the world—the so-called religious movements—can one do so without any prejudice, without taking any side, without projecting one's own personal conclusions, one's beliefs and dogmas, one's experience and knowledge and be totally free to observe clearly?

One may describe what compassion is in the most eloquent and poetic manner but in whatever words it is expressed, those words are not the thing. Without compassion there is no clarity; without

156

clarity there is no selfless skill—they are inter-related. Can one have this extraordinary sense of compassion in one's daily life, not as a theory, not as an ideal, not something to be achieved, to be practised and so on, but to have it totally, completely, at the very root of one's being?

Can there be clarity? One can be very clear in one's thinking, in its objectivity, rationality, sanity; but such thinking, however logical, however objective, is very limited. And one sees that such logical, objective thinking has not solved our problems; the philosophers, the scientists, the so-called religious people, have thought very clearly about certain things, but in daily life, clear thinking has not resolved our most important issues. One may think very clearly about one's envy or violence, but that does not bring about the ending of envy or violence. Clear thinking is limited because it is thought and thought itself is limited, conditioned. Thought itself has its own boundary; it may try to go beyond that boundary by inventing a logos, a deity or a Utopian State and so on, but these inventions are still limited because thought is the product of memory, experience and knowledge and it is always from the past and therefore time-bound. Is it possible to see the limitations of thought and give it its right place? Giving the right place to thought brings clarity.

To understand the whole meaning and the depth of compassion one has to investigate the movement of one's consciousness. Wherever one goes in the world, east or west, north or south, human beings have great anxiety and live in uncertainty, always seeking security in some form or another—physiologically or psychologically. And they are full of violence, right through the world; this is an extraordinary phenomenon—violence, greed, envy, hatred. In consciousness there is the good and the bad; the bad is increasing; it is increasing because the good has become static, the good is not flowering. One has accepted certain patterns of what is thought to be good and one lives according to those patterns. So, the good, instead of flowering, is withering and thereby giving strength to the bad. There is more violence, more hatred, there are more national and religious divisions, there is every form of antagonism, right through the world. It is on the increase because the good is not flowering. Now, be aware of this fact without any effort; the moment one makes effort one gives importance to the self, which is the bad. Just observe the actual fact of the bad without any effort, observe it without any choice—because choice is a distorting factor. When one observes so openly, so freely, then the good begins to flower. It is not that one pursues the good and thereby gives it strength to flower but when the bad, the evil, the ugly, is understood, completely, the other naturally flowers.

We have strengthened in our consciousness, through great development of skill, the structure and the nature of the self. The self is violence, the self is greed, envy and so on. They are of the very essence of the self. As long as there is the centre as the me, every action must be distorted. Acting from a centre you are giving a direction, and that direction is distortion. You may develop a great skill in this way but it is always unbalanced, inharmonious. Now, can consciousness with its movement undergo a radical transformation, a transformation not brought about by will? Will is desire, desire for something and when there is desire there is a motive, which is again a distorting factor in observation. In our consciousness there is this duality, the good and the bad. We are always looking with the eyes of the good and also with the eyes of the bad, so there is a conflict. Now to eliminate conflict altogether is only possible when you observe without any choice. Just observe yourself. In that way you eliminate the conflict between the good and the bad.

VI

Reason and logic alone
will not discover truth

Reason and logic have not solved our human problems, and we are going to find out if there is quite a different approach to all the problems and travails of life. We shall come upon something that is beyond reason; for reason has not solved any of our political, economic or social problems; nor has it solved the intimate human problems between two people. It becomes more and more obvious that we live in a world that is going to pieces, that has become quite insane, quite disorderly and a dangerous place to live in. Up to a point we must reason together, logically, sanely, holistically; then, perhaps, beyond that point, we shall be able to find a different state, a different quality of mind, not bound by any dogma, by any belief, by any experience and therefore a mind that is free to observe and through that observation see exactly "what is" and also find that there is energy to transform it.

One must not start from any conclusion, from any belief, from any dogma which conditions the mind, but from a mind that is free to observe, to learn, to move and act. Such a mind is a compassionate mind for compassion has no cause; it is not a result. Compassion comes when the mind is free and it brings about a fundamental psychological revolution. That psychological revolution is what we are concerned with from the beginning to the end.

So we will begin by asking ourselves: What is it that we are seeking? Physical comfort? Physical security? Deep down, is there the demand or desire to be totally secure in all our activities; in all our relationships to be stable, certain, permanent? We cling to experience that gives us a certain quality of stability, or to a certain identification which gives us a sense of permanency, well-being. In a belief there is security; in identification with a particular dogma, political or religious, there is security. If we are aged, we find security or happiness in the remembrance of things past, in the experiences that we have known, in the love that we have had, and we cling to the past. And if we are young and cheerful we are satisfied for the moment, not thinking about the future or the past. But gradually youth slips into old age with the desire to be secure, with the anxiety of uncertainty, of not being able to depend on anything or anybody, yet desiring deeply to have something secure to cling to.

We have to examine closely whether there is psychological security at all. And if there is no psychological security will a human being go insane; will he become totally neurotic, because he has no security? Probably the majority of human beings are somewhat neurotic. A Communist, a Catholic, Protestant or Hindu, each is secure in his belief; he has no fear because he clings to it. And when you begin to investigate, or question, or reason with him he stops at a certain point and will not examine further, it is too dangerous, he feels his security is being threatened; then communication ceases. He may reason, think logically up to a certain point but is incapable of breaking through to a different dimension altogether; he is stuck in a groove and will not investigate anything else. Does that really give security? Does thought, which has created all these beliefs, dogmas, experiences, divisions, give security? We function with thought; all our activity is based on thought, horizontal or vertical; whether you are aspiring to great heights it is the movement of thought vertically; or whether you are merely satisfied to bring about a social revolution and so on it is the horizontal movement of thought. So does thought fundamentally, basically, give security, psychologically? Thought has its place; but when thought assumes that it can bring about psychological security then it is living in illusion. Thought wanting ultimate security has created a thing called god; and humanity clings to that idea. Thought can create every kind of romantic illusion. And when the mind, psychologically, seeks security in the dogma of the Church, or some other dogmatic assertion, or whatever it is, it is seeking security in the structure of thought.

Thought is the response of experience and knowledge, stored up in the brain as memory; that response is therefore always moving from the past. Now, is there security in the past? Please use your reason, logic, all your energy to find out. Can any activity of thought, which is essentially of the past, give security? Follow the sequence of it; in that which it has created it seeks security and that security is of the past. Thought, though it may project the future, says: "I am going to attain godhood", yet that movement of thought is essentially from the past. Or, recognizing there is no security in the past, thought then projects an idea, an idealistic state of mind and finds security in the hope of that in the future.

A human being, throughout life, depends on thought and the things that thought has put together as being most essential, holiness, unholiness, morality, immorality and so on. Someone comes along and says: "Now look, all that is the movement of the past." Having reasoned with him, logically, the other says: "Why not, what is wrong with holding on to thought even though it is of the past?"; he acknowledges it, and says: "I'll hold to it, what is wrong?" Yet when the human mind lives in the past and when it holds to the past, then it is incapable of living, or perceiving truth.

We come to a certain point and we say: "Yes, I see and I recognize logically, that in those things there is no security and when they are questioned there is fear." And when we say we see that, what do we mean by that word "*see*"? Is it merely a logical understanding, a verbal understanding, a linear understanding, or is it an understanding which is so profound that that very understanding breaks down, without any effort, the whole movement of thought? When you say: "I understand what you are saying", what do you mean by that word "understand"? Do you mean you understand the English words? Is it an understanding of the words, the meaning of the words, the explanation of the words and therefore an understanding only at a very superficial level? Or, is it that, when you say "I understand", you mean you actually "*see*", or observe the truth as to what thought is; you actually feel, taste, observe in your blood as it were, that thought, whatever it creates, has no security? You "see" the truth of it and therefore you are free of it. Seeing the truth of it is intelligence. Such intelligence is not reason, logic, or the very careful dialectical explanation; the latter is merely the exposition of thought in various forms; and thought is never intelligent. The perception of the truth is intelligence; and in that intelligence there is complete security. That intelligence is not yours or mine; that intelligence is not conditioned—we have finished with all that. We have seen that thought in its very movement creates conditioning and when you understand that movement, that very understanding is intelligence. In that intelligence there is security, from that there is action.

We may talk about this question in different ways, in different fields, such as fear, pleasure, sorrow, death, meditation, but the essence of it is this: thought is the movement from the past, therefore of time and therefore measurable. That which is measurable can never find the immeasurable, which is truth. That can only take place when the mind actually sees the truth that whatever thought has created, in that there is no security; the very observation of that is intelligence. When there is that intelligence then it is all finished. Then you are out of this world, though you are living in it; though trying to do something in it, you are completely an outsider.

VII

Intelligence, in which there is complete security

Wherever one goes in the world, India, Europe and America, one sees great sorrow, violence, wars, terrorism, killing, drugs—every kind of stupidity. One accepts these as though inevitable and easily puts up with them, or one revolts against them; but revolt is a reaction, as Communism is a reaction to Capitalism or Fascism.

So, without revolting, without going against everything and forming one's own little group, or without following a guru from India or from elsewhere, without accepting any kind of authority—because in spiritual matters there is no authority—can we investigate these problems that human beings have had, centuries upon centuries, generation after generation, these conflicts, uncertainties, travails, all the things that human beings go through during life only to end in death, without understanding what it is all about?

Psychologically, inwardly, every human being, whoever he is, is the world. The world is represented in oneself and oneself is the world. That is a psychological, absolute fact; though one may have a white skin and another a brown or black skin, be affluent or very poor, yet inwardly, deep down, we are all the same; we suffer loneliness, sorrow, conflict, misery, confusion; we depend on someone to tell us what to do, how to think, what to think; we are slaves to propaganda from the various political parties and religions, and so on. That is what is happening all over the world inwardly; deep down, we are slaves to the propaganda of the experts, of the governments and so on, we are conditioned human beings, whether we live in India, Europe or America.

So, one is actually, psychologically, the world and the world is oneself. Once one realizes this fact, not verbally, not ideologically or as an escape from fact, but actually, deeply feel the fact, realize the fact, that one is not different from the other—however far away he is—inwardly he suffers greatly and is terribly frightened, uncertain, insecure, then one is not concerned with one's little self, one is concerned with the total human being. One is concerned with the total human being—not with Mr X or Y or somebody else—but with the total psychological entity as a human being, wherever he lives. He is conditioned in a particular way; he may be a Catholic, a Protestant, or he may be conditioned by thousands of years of certain kinds of beliefs, superstitions, ideas and gods, as in India, but below that conditioning, in the depth of his mind, when alone, he is facing the same life of sorrow, pain, grief and anxiety. When one sees this as an actual, irrevocable fact, then one begins to think entirely differently and one begins to observe, not as an individual person having troubles and anxieties, but whole, entire. It gives one an extraordinary strength and vitality; one is not alone, one is the entire history of mankind—if one knows how to read that history which is enshrined in one. This is not rhetoric but a serious factor one is deeply concerned with, a fact which one denies, because one thinks one is so individualistic. One is so concerned with oneself, with one's petty problems, with one's little guru, with one's little beliefs; but when one realizes this extraordinary fact, then it gives one tremendous strength and a great urgency to investigate and transform oneself, because one is mankind. When there is such transformation, one affects the whole consciousness of man because one is the entire humanity; when one changes fundamentally, deeply, when there is this psychological revolution in one, then naturally, as one is part of the total consciousness of the human being, which is the rest of humanity, its consciousness is affected. So, one is concerned to penetrate the layers of one's consciousness and to investigate whether it is possible to transform the content of that consciousness so that out of that transformation a different dimension of energy and clarity may come into being.

A human being, who is representative of the world, who is the world, psychologically, what is his innermost demand? In one part of his consciousness it is to find both biological and psychological security; he must have food, clothes and shelter—that is an absolute necessity. But also he demands, craves, and searches for psychological security—to have psychological certainty about everything. The whole struggle in the world, both physiologically and psychologically, is to find security.

Security means physical permanency, physically to be well, to continue, advance, grow, and also it means psychological permanency. Everything, psychologically, if one observes very carefully, is very impermanent; one's relationships, psychologically, are most uncertain. One may be temporarily secure in one's relationship with another, man or woman, but it is only temporary. That very temporary security is the ground of complete insecurity.

So one asks: is there any security, psychologically, at all? One seeks psychological security in the family—the family being the wife, the children. There one tries to find a relationship that will be secure, lasting, permanent—all relative, because there is always death. And, not always finding it—there are divorces, quarrels and all the misery, jealousies, anger, hatred that goes on—one tries to find security in a community, with a group of people, large or small. One tries to find security in the nation—I'm an American, I'm a Hindu—that gives a tremendous sense of apparent security. But when one tries to find security, psychologically, in a nation, that nation is divided from another nation. Where there is division between nations—in one of which one has invested psychologically one's security—there are wars, there are economic pressures. That is what is actually going on in the world.

If one seeks security in an ideology—the Communist ideology, the Capitalist ideology, the religious ideologies, with their dogmas, images—there is division; one believes in one set of ideals which one likes, which give one comfort, in which one seeks security with a group of people who believe the same thing, yet another group believes another thing and from them one is divided. Religions have divided people. The Christians, the Buddhists, the Hindus, the Muslims, divide; they are at each other, each believing something extraordinary, romantic, unrealistic, unreal, not factual.

Seeing all this—not as something to be avoided or to become supercilious or intellectual about—seeing all this very clearly, one asks, is there psychological security at all? And, if there is no psychological security, then does it become chaos? One loses one's identity—one has been identified with a nation, America, or with Jesus, with Buddha and so on—when reason, logic, makes it clear how absurd all this is. Does one despair because one has observed the fallacy of these divisive processes, the unreality of these fictions, myths, fantasies which have no basis? The very perception of all this is intelligence—not the intelligence of a clever, cunning mind, not the intelligence of book knowledge, but the intelligence which comes out of clear observation. In that intelligence, brought about this clear observation, there is security; that very intelligence is secure.

But one will not let go, one is too afraid to let go lest one does not find security. One can let go of being a Catholic, Protestant, Communist, and so on, fairly easily. But when one does let go, when one cleanses oneself of all this, either one does it as a reaction, or one does it because one has observed intelligently, holistically, with great clarity, the absurdity of the fantasies and the make-belief. Because one observes without any distortion, because one is not out to get something from it, because one is not thinking in terms of punishment and reward, because one observes very clearly, then that very clarity of perception is intelligence. In that there is extraordinary security—not that *you* become secure, but intelligence is secure.

One has come to the absolute fact—not relative fact—the absolute fact that there is no psychological security in anything that man has invented; one sees that all our religions are inventions, put together by thought. When one sees that all our divisive endeavours, which come about when there are beliefs, dogmas, rituals, which are the whole substance of religion, when one sees all that very clearly, not as an idea, but as a fact, then that very fact reveals the extraordinary quality of intelligence in which there is complete, whole security.

VIII

In negation the positive is born

We are dealing with the facts of daily life, our way of living. Most of us abstract from those facts ideas and conclusions which become our prisons. We may ventilate those prisons but still we live there and go on making further abstractions of facts there. We are not dealing with ideas, exotic philosophies, or with abstract conclusions. We are going into problems that require a great deal of care and about which we must be very serious—because the house is burning. The Communist world is pressing in all the time, constraining us to believe in certain ideologies and if we do not we can be sent either to a concentration camp or a mental hospital. That is gradually closing in. If you are aware of the world situation, of what is happening in the world economically, socially, politically, of the preparation for wars, you become extremely serious; it is not a thing to play around with, you have to act.

Most of us are mediocre—we just go half way up the hill. Excellence means going to the very top of it and we are asking for excellence. Otherwise we shall be smothered, destroyed, as human beings, by the politicians, by the ideologists, whether they are Communists, Socialists and so on. We are demanding of ourselves the highest form of excellence. That excellence can only come into being when there is clarity and compassion without which the human mind will destroy human beings, destroy the world.

We are exercising reason, clear objective thinking, and logic, but they themselves do not bring about compassion. We must exercise the qualities that we have, which are reason, careful observation and from those the excellency of clear sight to examine the various contents of consciousness, in which compassion does not exist; there may be pity in them, sympathy and tolerance, there may be the desire to help, there may be a form of love, but all these are not compassion.

Is compassion or love, pleasure? What is the significance and the meaning of pleasure, which every human being is seeking and pursuing at any cost? What is pleasure? There is the pleasure derived from possessions; the pleasure derived from a capacity or talent; the pleasure when you dominate another; the pleasure of having tremendous power, politically, religiously or economically; the pleasure of sex; the pleasure of the great sense of freedom that money gives. There are multiple forms of pleasure. In pleasure there is enjoyment, and further on there is ecstacy, the taking delight in something and the sense of ecstacy. "Ecstacy" is to be beyond yourself. There is no self to enjoy. The self—that is the me, the ego, the personality—has all totally disappeared, there is only that sense of being outside. That is ecstacy. But that ecstacy has nothing whatsoever to do with pleasure.

You take a delight in something; the delight that comes naturally when you look at something very beautiful. At that moment, at that second, there is neither pleasure, nor joy, there is only that sense of observation. In that observation the self is not. When you look at a mountain with its snow cap, with its valleys, its grandeur and magnificence, all thought is driven away. There it is, that greatness in front of you and there is delight. Then thought comes along registering as memory what a marvellous and lovely experience it was. Then that registration, that memory, is cultivated and that cultivation becomes pleasure. Whenever thought interferes with the sense of beauty, the sense of the greatness of anything, a piece of poetry, a sheet of water, or a lonely tree in a field, it is registration. But, to see it and not register it—that is important. The moment you register it, the beauty of it, then that very registration sets thought into action; then the desire to pursue that beauty, which becomes the pursuit of pleasure. One sees a beautiful woman, or man; instantly it is registered in the brain; then that very registration sets thought into motion and you want to be in her or his company and all that follows. Pleasure is the continuation and the cultivation in thought of a perception. You have had sexual experience last night, or two weeks ago, you remember it and desire the repetition of it, which is the demand for pleasure.

It is the function of the brain to register; in registration it is secure, it knows what to do and from that there is the development of skill. That skill in its turn becomes a great pleasure as a talent, a gift; it is the movement, the continuation, of thought through desire and pleasure.

Is it possible to register only that which is absolutely necessary and not register anything else? Take a very simple thing: most of us have had physical pain of some sort or another; that pain is registered and the brain says, tomorrow, or a week later, I must be very careful not to have that pain again. Physical pain is distorting; you cannot think clearly when there is great pain. It is the function of the brain to register that pain so as to safeguard itself from doing things that will bring about pain. It must register and then there is the fear of that pain happening again later—that registration has caused fear. Is it possible, having had that pain, to end it, not carry it on, not carry it over? If so, then the brain has the security of being free and intelligent; but the moment the pain is carried over it is never free.

Is it possible to register only the things that are absolutely necessary? The necessary things are the knowledge of how to drive a car, how to speak a language, technological knowledge, the knowledge of reading, writing and so on. But in our human relationships, those between man and woman for example, every incident in that relationship is registered. What takes place? The woman is irritated, nags, or is friendly, kindly, or says something just before the man goes off to the office, which is ugly; so from this there is built up, through registration, an image about her and she builds an image about him—this is factual. In human relationships, between man and woman, or between neighbours and so on, there is registration and the process of image making. But when the husband says something ugly listen to it carefully, end it, do not carry it on; then you will find that there is no image-making at all. If there is no image-making between a man and a woman the relationship is entirely different; there is no longer the relationship of one thought opposed to another thought—which is called relationship, which actually it is not; it is just ideas.

Pleasure follows registration of an incident in the continuation given by thought. Thought is the root of pleasure. If you had no thought and you saw a beautiful thing it would rest at that. But thought says: "No I must have that"; from this flows the whole movement of thought.

What is the relationship of pleasure to joy? Joy comes to you uninvited, it happens. You are walking along in a street, or sitting in a bus, or wandering in the woods, seeing the flowers, the hills, and the clouds and the blue sky and suddenly there is the extraordinary feeling of great joy; then comes the registration, thought says: "What a marvellous thing that was, I must have more of it." So, again, joy is made into pleasure by thought. This is seeing things as they are, not as you want them to be; it is seeing them exactly, without any distortion, seeing what is taking place.

What is love? Is it pleasure; which is the continuation of an incident through the movement of thought? Is the movement of thought love? Is love remembrance? A thing has happened and living in its remembrance, feeling that remembrance of something which is over, resuscitating it and saying, "What a marvellous thing that was when we were together under that tree; that was love"—all that is the remembrance of a thing that is gone. Is that love? Is love the pleasure of sex?—in which there is tenderness, kindliness and so on—is that love? That is not to say that it is, or that it is not.

We are questioning everything that man has put together of which he says: "This is love." If love is pleasure then it gives emphasis to the remembrance of past things and therefore brings about the importance of the me—my pleasure, my excitement, my remembrances. Is that love? And is love desire? What is desire? One desires a car; one desires a house; one desires prominence, power, position. There are infinite things one desires; to be as beautiful as you are; to be as intelligent, as clever, as smart as you are. Does desire bring clarity?

The thing that is called love is based on desire—desire to sleep with a woman, or sleep with a man, desire to possess her, dominate her, control her, "she is mine, not yours." Is love in the pleasure derived in that possession, in that dominance? Man dominates the world and now there is woman fighting the domination.

What is desire? Does desire bring about clarity? In its field does compassion flower? If it does not bring clarity and if desire is not the field in which the beauty and the greatness of compassion flower, then what place has desire? How does desire arise? One sees a beautiful woman, or a beautiful man—one sees. There is the perception, the seeing, then the contact, then the sensation, then that sensation is taken over by thought, which becomes the image with its desire. You see a beautiful vase, a beautiful sculpture—ancient Egyptian, or Greek—and you look at it and you touch it; you see the depth of sculpture of the figure sitting cross-legged. From that there is a sensation. What a marvellous thing

170

and from that sensation desire; "I wish I had that in my room; to look at it every day, touch it every day"—the pride of possession, to have such a marvellous thing as that. That is desire: seeing, contact, sensation, then thought using that sensation to cultivate the desire to possess—or not to possess.

Now comes the difficulty: realizing this the religious people have said: "Take vows of celibacy; do not look at a woman; if you do look treat her as your sister, mother, whatever you like; because you are in the service of God you need all your energy to serve Him; in the service of God you are going to have great tribulations, therefore be prepared, but do not waste your energy." But the thing is boiling and we are trying to understand that desire which is constantly boiling, wanting to fulfil, wanting to complete itself.

Desire arises from the movement—seeing—contact—sensation —thought with its image—desire. Now we are saying: seeing —touching—sensation, that is normal, healthy—end it there, do not let thought take it over and make it into a desire. Understand this and then you will also understand that there will be no suppression of desire. You see a beautiful house, well proportioned with lovely windows, a roof that melts into the sky, walls that are thick and part of the earth, a beautiful garden, well kept. You look at it, there is sensation; you touch it—you may not actually touch it but you touch it with your eyes—you smell the air, the herbs, the newly-cut grass. Can you not end it there? End it there, say: "It is a beautiful house"; but there is no registration and no thought which says: "I wish I had that house"—which is desire and the continuation of desire. You can do this so easily; and I mean easily, if you understand the nature of thought and desire.

Is thought love? Does thought cultivate love? It is not pleasure, it is not desire, it is not remembrance, although they have their places. Then what is love? Is love jealousy? Is love a sense of possession, my wife, my husband, my girl—possession? Has love within it fear? It is none of these things, entirely wipe them all away, end them, putting them all in their right place—then love is.

Through negation the positive is—through negation; that is: is pleasure love?—you examine pleasure and see it is not that —though pleasure has its place it is not that—so you negate that. You see it is not remembrance though remembrance is necessary; so put remembrance in its right place, therefore you have negated remembrance as not being love. You have negated desire, though

171

desire has a certain place. Therefore through negation the positive is. But we, on the contrary, posit the positive and then get caught in the negative. One must begin with doubt—completely doubting—then you end up with certainty. But if you start with certainty, then you end up in uncertainty and chaos.

So in negation the positive is born.

IX

Because there is space, there is emptiness and total silence

Time, for us, is very important, both chronologically and psychologically. We depend so much on psychological time. Time is related to movement—from here to there takes time. A distance to be covered, to arrive at a goal, to fulfil a purpose, requires time. To learn a language requires time. That has been carried over into the psychological field: "We need time to be perfect; we need time to get over something; we need time to be free of our anxieties; to be free of our sorrow; to be free of our fears and so on." Time is needed in practical matters, in the field of technology and so on and that need for time has been introduced into our psychological life and we have accepted it. To wipe away our nationalities, to become brotherly we think we need time. Psychological time implies hope; the world is mad, let us hope in the future there will be a sane world. We are questioning whether there is such a thing as psychological time at all. We ask: Is there an action in which time is not involved at all? Action arising from a cause, a motive, needs time. Action based on a pattern of memory needs time to put into action. If you have an ideal, however noble, however beautiful and romantic, however nonsensical even, you need time to arrive at that idealistic state. And to arrive at that you destroy the present. It does not matter what happens to you now; what is important is the future. For the sake of the future sacrifice yourself now—some marvellous future established by the ideologists, the religious teachers and so on throughout the world. We question that and ask whether there is any psychological time at all and therefore no hope. "What shall I do if I have no hope?" Hope is so important because it gives you satisfaction, energy, drive to achieve something.

When one looks closely, non-sentimentally, logically, is there psychological time at all? There is psychological time only when one moves away from "what is". There is psychological time when one realizes that one is violent and then proceeds to enquire how to be free of it; that movement away from "what is" is time. But if one is totally and completely aware of "what is", then there is no such time.

Most of us are violent. Violence is not only hitting somebody physically, but anger, jealousy, acceptance of authority, conformity, imitation, accepting the edicts of another. Human beings are violent; that is the fact—violence. The very word "violence" condemns it. By the very usage of the word "violence" you have already condemned violence. See the intricacies of this. Being violent and being negligent, or lazy, we move away from it and invent ideological non-violence. That is time—the movement from "what is" to "what should be". That time comes to an end, completely, when there is only "what is"—which is non-verbal identification with "what is". Anger is a form of violence, or hatred, jealousy. The words "anger", "hatred" or "jealousy" in themselves are condemnatory; they are verbalizations which strengthen by reaction. When I say "I am angry," I have recognized from past angers the present anger, so I am using the word "anger" which is of the past and identifying that word with the present. The word has become extraordinarily important; yet if there is no usage of the word so that there is only the fact, the reaction, then there is no strengthening of that feeling.

Is it possible to live, psychologically, without tomorrow? To say: "I love you, I will meet you tomorrow", that affection is in memory projected towards tomorrow. Is there an activity without time at all? Love is not time; it is not a remembrance. If it is, it is not love, obviously. "I love you because you gave me sex; or you gave me food, or flattered me; or you said you needed a companion; I am lonely therefore I need you"—all that is not love, surely? When there is jealousy, when there is anxiety or hatred, that is not love. So then what is love? Love is obviously a state of mind in which there is no verbalization, no remembrance, but something immediate.

There is a way of living, in daily life, where time as movement from this state to that, has gone. What happens when you do that? You have an extraordinary vitality, an extraordinary sense of clarity. You are then only dealing with facts, not with ideas. But as most of us are imprisoned in ideas and have accepted that way of life, it is very difficult to break away. But, have an insight into it, then it is finished.

Our minds are so cluttered up, with knowledge, with worries, with problems, with money, with position and prestige; they are so burdened that there is no space at all; yet without space there is no order.

When I look at this valley from a height and there is a direction because I want to see where I live, then I lose the vastness of space. Where there is direction space is limited. Where there is a purpose, a goal, something to be achieved, there is no space. If you have a purpose in life for which you are living, concentrating, where is there space? Whereas if there is no concentration there is vast space.

When there is a centre from which we look, then space is very limited. When there is no centre, that is to say, no structure of the me which has been put together by thought, there is vast space. Without space there is no order, there is no clarity, there is no compassion.

Living where there is no effort, where there is no action of will, where there is tremendous space, is part of meditation.

So far we have only dealt with the waves on the surface of the ocean. You have only dealt with the superficiality of it. Now, if you have gone so far you can go into the depth of the ocean—of course you must understand how to dive deeply; not *you* dive—it comes about.

There is concentration, choiceless awareness and attention. Concentration implies resistance. Concentration on a particular thing, on the page you are reading, or on the phrase you are trying to understand: to concentrate is to put all your energy in a particular direction. In concentration there is resistance and therefore effort and division. You want to concentrate, thought goes off on something else, you bring it back—the fight. If you are interested in something you concentrate very easily. Implied in the word concentrate is putting your mind on a particular object, a particular picture, a particular action.

Choiceless awareness is to be aware both externally and inwardly, without any choice. Just to be aware of the trees, the mountains, nature—just to be aware. Not choose, saying, "I like this", "I don't like that", or "I want this", "I don't want that". It

175

is to observe without the observer. The observer is the past, which is conditioned, always looking from that conditioned point of view, therefore there is like and dislike and so on. To be choicelessly aware implies observing the whole environment around you, the mountains, the trees, also the ugly world and the towns; just to be aware, observe and in that observation there is no decision, no will, no choice.

In attention there is no centre, there is no me attending. When there is no me which limits attention then attention is limitless; attention has limitless space.

After understanding all the waves on the surface—fear, authority, all the petty affairs compared to that which we are going into—the mind has then emptied consciousness of the whole of its content. It is empty; not through action of will, not through desire, not through choice. Consciousness, then, is totally different, is of a totally different dimension.

Because there is space there is emptiness and total silence—not induced silence, not practised silence; which are all just the movement of thought and therefore absolutely worthless. When you have gone through all this—and there is great delight in going through all this, it is like playing a tremendous game—then in that total silence there is a movement which is timeless, which is not measured by thought—thought has no place in it whatsoever—then there is something totally sacred, timeless.

X

The state of the mind that has insight is completely empty

An awakened intelligence has a deep, true, insight into all our psychological problems, crises, blockages and so on; not intellectual comprehension, not the resolving of problems through conflict. Having an insight into a human issue is to awaken this intelligence; or, having this intelligence, there is the insight—both ways. In such insight there is no conflict; when you see something very clearly, when you see the truth of the matter, there is the end of it, you do not fight against it, you do not try to control, you do not make all manner of calculated, motivated, efforts. From that insight, which is intelligence, there is action—not postponed action but immediate action.

We are educated from childhood to exercise, as deeply as possible, every form of effort. If you observe yourself you will see what tremendous efforts we make to control ourselves, to suppress, adjust and modify ourselves to certain patterns or objectives that you or another have established; so there is constant struggle. We live with it and we die with it. And we ask: Is it possible to live our daily life without a single conflict?

Most of us are awakened to all the problems, political, religious, economic, social, ideological and so on, in which we live. Being somewhat aware of all that most of us are discontent. When you are young, this dissatisfaction becomes like a flame and you have a passion to do something. So you join some political party, the extreme Left, the extreme revolutionary, the extreme forms of "Jesus freaks" and so on and so on. By joining these things, by adopting certain attitudes, certain ideologies, that flame of discontent fades away and you then appear to be satisfied. You say: "This is what I want to do" and you pour your heart into it. But gradually you find, if you are at all awake to the problems involved, that you are not satisfied. It is too late; you have already given half your life to something which you thought would be completely worthwhile and you have found later on that it is not so; then your energy, capacity and drive has withered away. Gradually the real flame of discontent has withered away. You must have noticed the pattern that has been followed all the time, generation after generation, in yourself, in your children, in the young and the old.

But if you are alive to all these things and are discontented and if you do not allow this discontent to be squashed by the desire to be satisfied, by the desire to adjust oneself to the environment, to the "establishment", or to an ideal, to a Utopia, if you allow this flame to keep on burning, not being satisfied with anything, then the superficial satisfactions have no place; then this very dissatisfaction is demanding something much greater and the ideals, the gurus, the religions, the "establishment", become totally superficial. The flame of discontent, because it has no outlet, because it has no object in which it can fulfil itself, that flame becomes a great passion. That passion is intelligence. If you are not caught in these superficial, essentially reactionary things, then that extraordinary flame is intensified. That intensity brings about a quality of mind having a deep insight instantly into things, and from that there is action.

Such dissatisfaction does not make you neurotic or bring about imbalance. There is imbalance only when this dissatisfaction is translated, or caught in a trap of some kind or another; then there is distortion, then there are all kinds of fights, inwardly.

If you have been caught in these various traps, can you put them aside, wipe them out, destroy them?—do what you like, but have this tremendous flame of discontent *now*. It does not mean that you throw bombs at people, destroy, indulge in physical revolution and riots. When you put aside all the traps that man has created around you and that you have created for yourself, then this flame becomes a supreme intelligence. And that intelligence gives you insight. And when you have insight, from that there is immediate action.

Action is not tomorrow. There is an action without cause; it has been a problem for many great thinkers; action without cause, action without motive, action not dependent on some ideology. One of the demands of serious people is to find out if there is an action which is *per se*, for itself; which is without cause and motive. See what is implied in it: no regrets, no retention of those regrets and all the sequence that follows from those regrets, such action does not depend on some past or future ideology; it is an action which is always free. It is an action that is only possible when there is insight born of intelligence.

Most people would say that there must be conflict otherwise there is no growth; that conflict is part of life. A tree in a forest struggles to reach the sun; that is a form of conflict. Every animal is in conflict. And we human beings, supposed to be intelligent, are yet constantly in conflict. Now discontent says: "Why should I be in conflict?" Conflict implies comparison, imitation, conformity, adjustment to a pattern, the modified continuity of what has been, through the present, to the future—all a process of conflict. The deeper the conflict the more neurotic you become. And so, in order to have respite from conflict you believe most deeply in God, saying: "His will be done"—and we create this monstrous world.

Conflict implies comparison. Can one live without comparison?—which means no ideal, no authority of a pattern, no conformity to a particular ideology. It implies freedom from the prison of ideas so that there is no comparison, no imitation, no conformity; therefore you are stuck with "what is"—actually what is. Comparison comes only when you compare "what is" with "what should be", or "what might be", or try to transform "what is" into something which it is not and all this implies conflict.

To live without comparison is to remove a tremendous burden. If you remove the burden of comparison, imitation, conformity, adjustment, modification, then you are left with "what is". Conflict arises only when you try to do something with "what is", try to transform it, to modify it, to change it, or to suppress it, run away from it. But if you have an insight into "what is" then conflict ceases; you are left with "what is". And what happens to "what is"? What is the state of your mind when you are looking at "what is"? What is the state of your mind when you are not escaping, not trying to transform, or deform "what is"? What is the state of that mind that is looking and has insight? The state of the mind that has insight is completely empty. It is free from escapes, free from suppression, analysis and so on. When all these burdens are taken away—because you see the absurdity of them, it is like taking away a heavy burden—there is freedom. Freedom implies an emptiness to observe. That emptiness gives you insight into violence—not the various forms of violence, but the whole nature of violence and the structure of violence; therefore there is immediate action about violence, which is to be free, completely, from all violence.

XI

Where there is suffering you cannot
possibly love

We say that love is part of suffering. When you love somebody it brings about suffering. We are going to question whether it is possible to be free of all suffering. When there is freedom from suffering in the consciousness of the human being then that freedom brings about a transformation in consciousness and that transformation affects the whole of mankind's suffering. That is part of compassion.

Where there is suffering you cannot possibly love. That is a truth, a law. When you love somebody and he or she does something of which you totally disapprove and you suffer, it shows that you do not love. See the truth of it. How can you suffer when your wife throws you away and goes after somebody else? Yet we suffer from that. We get angry, jealous, envious, hateful; at the same time we say, "I love my wife"! Such love is not love. So, is it possible not to suffer and yet have the flowering of immense love?

What is the nature and the essence of suffering—the essence of it, not the various forms of it? What is the essence of suffering? Is it not the total expression, at that moment, of complete self-centred existence? It is the essence of the me—the essence of the ego, the person, the limited, enclosed, resisting existence, which is called the "me". When there is an incident that demands understanding and insight, that is denied by the awakening of the me, the essence which is the cause of suffering. If there were no me, would there be suffering? One would help, one would do all kinds of things, but one would not suffer.

Suffering is the expression of the me; it includes self-pity, loneliness, trying to escape, trying to be with the other who is gone—and all else that is implied. Suffering is the very me, which is the image, the knowledge, the remembrance of the past. So, what relationship

181

has suffering, the essence of the me, to love? Is there any relationship between love and suffering? The me is put together by thought: but is love put together by thought?

Is love put together by thought?—the memories of the pains, the delights, and the pursuit of pleasure, sexual or otherwise, of the pleasure of possessing somebody and somebody liking to be possessed; all that is the structure of thought. The me with its name, with its form, its memory, is put together by thought—obviously. But if love is not put together by thought, then suffering has no relationship to love. Therefore action from love is different from action from suffering.

What place has thought in relation to love and in relation to suffering? To have an insight into it means you are neither escaping, wanting comfort, frightened to be lonely, isolated; it means therefore your mind is free and that which is free is empty. If you have that emptiness you have an insight into suffering. Then suffering as the me disappears. There is immediate action because that is so; action then is from love, not from suffering.

One discovers that action from suffering is the action of the me and that therefore there is constant conflict. One can see the logic of it all, the reason for it. Only so is it possible to love without a shadow of suffering. Thought is not love; thought is not compassion. Compassion is intelligence—which is not the outcome of thought. What is the action of intelligence? If one has intelligence it is operating, it is functioning, it is acting. But if one asks: What is the action of intelligence?—one merely wants *thought* to be satisfied. When one asks: What is the action of compassion?—is it not thought that is asking? Is it not the me that is saying: If I could have this compassion I would act differently? Therefore when one puts such questions one is still caught in terms of thought. But with an insight into thought then thought has its right place and intelligence then acts.

XII

Sorrow is the outcome of time and thought

We are concerned with the whole existence of man and whether a human being can ever be free from his travail, his efforts, his anxieties, violence and brutality, and whether there is an end to sorrow.

Why have human beings, throughout the ages, sustained and put up with suffering? Can there be an ending to it all?

One must be free of all ideologies. Ideologies are dangerous illusions, whether they are political, social, religious, or personal. Every form of ideology either ends up in totalitarianism, or in religious conditioning—as the Catholic, the Protestant, the Hindu, the Buddhist and so on; and ideologies become such great burdens. So, to go into the enormous question of suffering, one must be free from all ideologies. One may have experienced a great deal of suffering which may have brought about certain definite conclusions. But to enquire into this question one must be utterly free of all conclusions.

Obviously there is biological, physical, suffering, and that suffering may distort the mind if one is not very careful. But we are concerned with the psychological suffering of man. In investigating suffering we are investigating the suffering of all mankind, because each one of us is of the essence of all humanity; each one of us is, psychologically, inwardly, deeply, like the rest of mankind. They suffer, they go through great anxiety, uncertainty, confusion, violence, through great sense of grief, loss, loneliness, as each one of us does. There is no division, psychologically, between us all. We are the world, psychologically, and the world is us. That is not a conviction, that is not a conclusion, that is not an intellectual theory, but an actuality, to be felt, to be realized and to be lived. Investigating this question of sorrow one is investigating not only one's own personal limited sorrow but also the sorrow of mankind. Do not reduce it to a personal thing, because when one sees the enormous suffering of mankind, in the understanding of the enormity of it, the wholeness of it, then one's own part has a rôle in it. It is not a selfish enquiry concerned with how I am to be free of sorrow. If one makes it personal, limited, then one will not understand the full significance of the enormity of sorrow.

In opposition to sorrow there is happiness, as in one's consciousness there is the bad and the good. In one's consciousness there is sorrow and a sense of happiness. In enquiring one is not concerned with sorrow as an opposite to happiness, gladness, enjoyment but with sorrow itself. The opposites contain each other. If the good is the outcome of the bad, then the good contains the bad. And if sorrow is the opposite of happiness, then the enquiry into sorrow has its root in happiness. We are enquiring into sorrow *per se*, not as an opposite to something else.

It is important to understand how one observes the nature and the movement of sorrow. How does one look at one's sorrow? If one looks at it as though it was different from oneself then there is a division between oneself and that which one calls sorrow. But is that sorrow different from oneself? Is the observer of sorrow different from sorrow itself? Or is it that the observer is sorrow? It is not that he is free from sorrow and then looks at sorrow, or identifies with sorrow. Sorrow is not just in the field of the observer; he is sorrow. The observer is the observed. The experiencer is the experienced; just as the thinker is the thought. There is no division as when the observer says "I am in sorrow", and who then divides himself off and tries to do something about sorrow—run away from it; seek comfort; suppress it; and all the various means of attempting to transcend sorrow. Whereas, if one sees that the observer is the observed, which is a fact, then one eliminates altogether the division that brings about conflict. One has been brought up, educated, to think that the observer is something totally different from the observed; as for example: one is the analyser therefore one can analyse—but the analyser is the analysed. So in this perception there is no division between the observer and the observed, between the thinker and the thought—there is no thought without the thinker—if there is no thinker there is no thought—they are one.

So if one sees that the observer is the observed, then one is not dictating what sorrow is, one is not telling sorrow what it should

184

be, or not be, one is just observing without any choice, without any movement of thought.

There are various kinds of sorrow; the man who has no work; the man who will always remain poor, the man who will never enjoy clean clothes or a fresh bath—as happens among the poor. There is the sorrow of ignorance, the sorrow when children are maltreated, the sorrow when animals are killed—vivisection and so on. There is the sorrow of war, which affects the whole of mankind. There is the sorrow when someone whom you love, dies. There is the sorrow of the desire to fulfil and the ensuing failure and frustration. So, there are multiple kinds of sorrow. Does one deal with all the multiple expressions of sorrow piecemeal? Or does one deal with the root of sorrow as a whole? Does one take each expression of the hundreds of varieties of sorrow? Or go to the very root of sorrow? If one takes all the multiple expressions of sorrow there will be no end. One may trim them individually, diminish them, but more will always remain. Can one look at the multiple branches of sorrow and through that observation go into the very root of sorrow, from the outside go inside and examine what is at the root, the cause? If one does not end sorrow there is no love in one's heart—although one may pity others and be troubled by the slaughter that is going on.

What is sorrow? Why does one suffer? Is it that one has lost something that one had? Or is there suffering because one has been promised a reward and that reward has not been given?—because we are educated through reward and punishment. Does one suffer because of self-pity? Because one has not the things that another has? Does one suffer through comparison, measurement? Does one suffer because, through limitation, one has not been able to achieve that which one is trying to imitate—trying to conform to a pattern and never reaching that pattern fully, completely? So one asks very deeply: What is suffering and why does one suffer?

One must be very careful in examination to see whether the word "sorrow" itself weighs down on man. Sorrow has been praised, romanticized. It has been made into something that is essential in order to find reality—one must go through suffering to find love, pity, compassion. We seek through suffering a reward. Does not the word "sorrow" bring about the feeling of sorrow? Or, independent of that word and the stimulation of that word, the reaction of that word, is there sorrow by itself?

If this examination is a matter of tremendous crisis in one's life, as it must be, then, when there is sorrow, it is a challenge and all one's energy is brought into being—otherwise one dissipates that energy by running away, seeking comfort, inventing explanations such as karma and so on. It is a challenge: What is sorrow? Is there an ending to sorrow? One can only respond completely to it when one has no fear, when one is not caught up in the machinery of pleasure, when one is not escaping from it, seeking comfort, but responding to it with all one's energy—a response that is the expression of the totality of one's energy.

In the understanding of the cause of sorrow does sorrow disappear? I may say to myself: "I am full of self-pity, if I can end self-pity there will be no sorrow." So I work at getting rid of it because I see how silly it is; I try to suppress it; I worry about it like a dog with a bone. And I may, intellectually, think I am free from sorrow. But the uncovering of the cause of sorrow is not the ending of sorrow. The searching for the cause of sorrow is a wastage of energy; sorrow is there, demanding one's tremendous attention. It is a challenge asking one to act. But instead of that one says: "Let me look to the cause; let me find out; is it this, that, or the other? I may be mistaken; let me talk it over with others; or is there some book that will tell me what the real cause is?" But all this is moving away from the actual fact, the actual response to that challenge.

If one's mind, the movement of its thought, is looking through its memory and responding according to that memory, according to previous knowledge, then one is acting not directly to the challenge, but merely responding from memory, from the past. I am in sorrow, my son, my wife, or the social conditions—the poverty, the brutality of man—bring about a great sorrow in me. It wants a response, a complete response, from me as a human being who represents the totality of humanity. If thought responds to the challenge saying: "I must find out how to respond to it; I have had sorrow before and I know all the meaning of the suffering and the pain, the anxiety and the loneliness of sorrow," then it is responding according to remembrance, therefore it is not an actual response; it is not actually seeing the fact that any response to that challenge from memory is no response at all, it is mere reaction. It is not action, it is reaction. Once see that, then the question is: What is the root of it all—not the cause? When there is a cause there is an effect and the effect in turn becomes a cause and the action from that becomes the cause for the next action. There is a chain effect. When the mind is caught in this limited chain, and it is always limited, then any response to the challenge will be very limited and time bound. But can one act to that challenge without a time interval? One may not actually have had any immediate sorrow, but one sees the enormity of the sorrow of mankind—the global sorrow of mankind. If one responds to that according to one's conditioning, according to one's past memory, then one is caught in action that is always time binding. The challenge and its response demand no time interval. Therefore there is instant action.

Fear is the movement of thought—thought as measure. Fear is time. Thought is the response of memory, knowledge, experience; it is limited; it is a movement in time. If there is no time there is no fear. I am living now but I am afraid I might die—I might in the future. There is a time interval produced by thought. But if there is no time interval at all, there is no fear. So, in the same way: is the root of sorrow time?—time being the movement of thought. And if there is no thought at all, when one responds to that challenge, is there suffering?

Can one put away, for the time being, all one's habitual ideas about time, sorrow and fear? Put away all one's conclusions, all that one has read about sorrow and begin again as though one knew nothing about sorrow. Though one suffers one has no answer to it. But one has been so conditioned: put the burden of sorrow on to somebody else, as Christianity has done so beautifully; go to church and one sees all the suffering in that figure. The Christians have given all that suffering over to somebody and think by that they have understood the whole vast field of sorrow. In India, in the Asiatic countries, they have also another form of eva-sion—karma. But face the actual movement at the moment of sorrow and be completely choicelessly aware of that thing and one asks: Is time, which is thought, the fundamental issue that makes sorrow flower? Is thought responsible for suffering?—not only the suffering of others, the brutality of others, but for the total ignor-ance of this whole earth.

There is no new thought; there is no free thought. There is only thought and that is the response of knowledge and experience, stored up in the brain as memory. Now if that is fact, if one sees that it is true that sorrow is the outcome of time and thought—if that is not a supposition—then one is responding to sorrow without the me for the me is put together by thought. My name, my form, how I look, my qualities, my reactions, all the things that are acquired, are all put together by thought. Thought is 'me'. Time is 'me', the self, the ego, the personality, all that is the movement of time as me. When there is no time, when one responds to this challenge of suffering and there is no me, then, is there suffering?

Is not all sorrow based on me, the individual, the personality, the ego? It is the self that says, "I suffer", "I am lonely", "I am anxious", this whole movement, this whole structure, is me in thought. And thought posits not only me but also that I am a superior me—something far superior to thought; yet it is still the movement of thought. So, there is an ending to sorrow when there is no me.

XIII

What is death?

One has known of thousands of deaths—the death of someone very close or the death of masses through the atomic bomb—Hiroshima and all the horrors that man has perpetrated on other human beings in the name of peace and in the pursuit of ideologies. So, without any ideology, without any conclusion, one asks: What is death? What is the thing that dies—that terminates? One sees that if there is something that is continuous it becomes mechanical. If there is an ending to everything there is a new beginning. If one is afraid then one cannot possibly find out what this immense thing called death is. It must be the most extraordinary thing. To find out what death is one must also enquire into what life is before death. One never does that. One never enquires what living is. Death is inevitable; but what is living? Is this living, this enormous suffering, fear, anxiety, sorrow, and all the rest of it—is this living? Clinging to that one is afraid of death. If one does not know what living is one cannot know what death is—they go together. If one can find out what the full meaning of living is, the totality of living, the wholeness of living, then one is capable of understanding the wholeness of death. But one usually enquires into the meaning of death without enquiring into the meaning of life.

When one asks: What is the meaning of life?—one immediately has conclusions. One says it is this; one gives it a significance according to one's conditioning. If one is an idealist, one gives life an ideological significance; again, according to one's conditioning, according to what one has read and so on. But if one is not giving a particular significance to life, if one is not saying life is this or something else, then one is free, free of ideologies, of systems, political, religious or social. So, before one enquires into the meaning of death one is asking what living is. Is the life one is living, living? The constant struggle with each other? Trying to understand each other? Is living according to a book, according to some psychologists, according to some orthodoxy, living?

If one banishes all that, totally, then one will begin with "what is". "What is" is that our living has become a tremendous torture, a tremendous battle between human beings, man, woman, neighbour—whether close or far. It is a conflict in which there is occasional freedom to look at the blue sky, to see something lovely and enjoy it and be happy for a while; but the cloud of struggle soon returns. All this we call living; going to church with all the traditional repetition, or the new English repetition, accepting certain ideologies. This is what one calls living and one is so committed to it one accepts it. But discontentment has its significance—real discontent. Discontent is a flame and one suppresses it by childish acts, by momentary satisfactions; but discontent when you let it flower, arise, it burns away everything that is not true.

Can one live a life that is whole, not fragmented?—a life in which thought does not divide as the family, the office, the church, this and that and death so divided off that when it comes one is appalled by it, one is shocked by it so that one's mind is incapable of meeting it because one has not lived a total life.

Death comes and with that one cannot argue; one cannot say: "Wait a few minutes more"—it is there. When it comes, can the mind meet the end of everything while one is living, while one has vitality and energy, while one is full of life? When one's life is not wasted in conflicts and worries one is full of energy, clarity. Death means the ending of all that one knows, of all one's attachments, of one's bank accounts, of all one's attainments—there is a complete ending. Can the mind, while living, meet such a state? Then one will understand the full meaning of what death is. If one clings to the idea of 'me', that me which one believes must continue, the me that is put together by thought, including the me in which one believes there is the higher consciousness, the supreme consciousness, then one will not understand what death is in life.

Thought lives in the known; it is the outcome of the known; if there is not freedom from the known one cannot possibly find out what death is, which is the ending of everything, the physical organism with all its ingrained habits, the identification with the body, with the name, with all the memories it has acquired. One cannot carry it all over when one goes to death. One cannot carry there all one's money; so, in the same way one has to end in life everything that one knows. That means there is absolute aloneness; not loneliness but aloneness, in the sense there is nothing else but that state of mind that is completely whole. Aloneness means all one.

XIV

That emptiness is the
summation of all energy

One's consciousness, which is oneself, is filled with one's own concepts and conclusions and with other people's ideas; it is filled with one's fears, anxieties and pleasures and with occasional flashes of joy and with one's sorrow. That is one's consciousness. That is the pattern of one's existence.

Is it at all possible to bring about a radical change in one's consciousness? For if it is not possible then one is everlastingly living in a prison of one's own ideas, one's own concepts—living in a field where there is every kind of confusion, uncertainty, instability. And one seems to think that if one moves from one corner of that field to another one has greatly changed, but still one is in the same field. As long as one lives within the field that one calls one's consciousness, however little or however great it may change, yet in that field there is no fundamental human transformation.

Ideologies, however clever, however carefully thought out, ultimately bring about dangerous illusions—whether they are the ideologies of the Right, Centre, or the extreme Left, they all end up either in great bureaucracies controlling man, or in concentration camps, or the destructive moulding of man according to a particular concept. This is what is happening throughout the world; the intellectuals have led us to this point.

We have been prisoners of religious ideologies and dogmas—the Catholic, the Hindu, the Buddhist and so on, and the gurus, with their modern modifications of the ancient traditions and ideologies, are also the prisoners of those ideologies.

If one observes all this, carefully, impersonally, objectively, one realizes that one must put away all ideologies and ask oneself whether consciousness with its content—which is what one is, with all one's conflicts, struggles, confusions, misery and occasional happiness—can become aware of itself and empty itself? That is one problem in meditation.

Meditation is not seeking an end; it is not groping purposefully after a goal. Out of meditation comes immense silence; not cultivated silence, not the silence between two thoughts, between two noises, but a silence that is unimaginable. The brain becomes extraordinarily quiet when in this process of enquiry; when there is silence there is great perception. In this silence there is emptiness, an emptiness that is the summation of all energy.

In examining the question of consciousness and its content it is very important to find out whether one, oneself, is observing it, or if in observing, consciousness becomes aware of itself. There is a difference. Either, one observes the movement of one's consciousness—one's desires, hurts, ambitions, greeds and all the rest of the content of our consciousness—as if from the outside; or consciousness becomes aware of itself. This is only possible when thought realizes that it is only observing what it has created, which is the content of its consciousness; then thought realizes that it is only observing itself, not 'me' which thought has put together observing consciousness. There is only observation; then consciousness begins to reveal its content, not only the superficial consciousness but the deeper layers of consciousness, the whole content of consciousness. If one sees the importance of sheer absolute motionless observation, then the thing flowers; consciousness opens up its doors.

One learns the art of observing without any distortion, without any motive, without any purpose—just to observe. In that there is tremendous beauty because then there is no distortion. One sees things clearly as they are. But if one makes an abstraction of them into ideas and then through the ideas observes, then it is a distortion.

One freely, without any distorting factor, enters into the observation of consciousness. There is nothing hidden and consciousness begins to reveal its own totality, its content, one's hurts, greed, envy, happiness, beliefs, ideologies, past traditions, the present scientific or factual traditions and so on and so on—all that is our consciousness. One observes it without any movement of thought; because it is thought that has put together all the content of our consciousness—thought has built it. When thought comes and says: "This is right, this is wrong, this shouldn't be, that should", one is still within the field of consciousness; one is not going beyond it. One has to understand very clearly the place of thought; it has its own place, in the field of knowledge, technology and so on. But thought has no place whatsoever in the psychological structure of man. So, can one observe one's consciousness and does it reveal its content?—not bit by bit, but the totality of its movement. Then only is it possible to go beyond it.

In enquiring, can one observe without any movement of the eye? Because the eye has an effect on the brain. When one keeps the eyeballs completely still observation becomes very clear because the brain is quietened. So, can one observe without any movement of thought interfering with one's observation? It is only possible when the observer realizes that he and that which he is observing are one—the observer is the observed. Anger is not different from me—I am anger, I am jealousy. There is no division between the observer and the observed; that is the basic reality one must capture. Then the whole of consciousness begins to reveal itself without the making of any effort. In that total observation there is the emptying of, or the going beyond, all the things that thought has put together—which is one's consciousness.

Then there is the problem of time—time psychologically, as a movement towards the fulfilment of an idea, an ideology. One is greedy, or violent: one says to oneself: "I will take time to get over it, or to modify it, or change it, or to get rid of it, or to go beyond it." That time is psychological time, not chronological time, by the watch or by the sun. There is this whole conditioning of one's mind which says: "I will take time to achieve that which I consider to be essential, to be beautiful, to be good." One questions that time, and asks: Is there psychological time at all? Is it not that thought has invented that time?

This is a very important thing to understand because it shatters altogether the idea of tomorrow—psychologically. It is a tremendous fact. If one understands that, psychologically, there is no tomorrow, then what will one do with that "which is"? If there is no time, then how is violence to end? One is conditioned to use time as a means of getting rid, slowly or quickly, of—say—violence. But if there is no time at all then what takes place when there is violence? Will there be violence? If it is one's whole outlook that, psychologically, there is no time at all, then is there a me who is violent? The me is put together through time. The me as violence, is time. But if there is no time at all as me, then there is nothing, there is no violence.

If there is no time at all, there is no past or future, but only something else, totally different. One is so conditioned to time and one says psychologically, that there must be time for me to evolve, for me to become something other than that which I am. When one sees the truth of the fact that thought itself is the cause of this time, then there is an ending of the past and the future; there is only the sense of timeless movement now. It is really extraordinary if one understands this. And, after all, love is that. Love is at the same level, at the same time, at the same intensity; at that moment that is love—not the remembrance of it, or the future hope for it. That state of mind, which is love, is really completely without time. Then see what happens in one's relationship with another. One perhaps has that extraordinary sense of love which is not of time, which is not of thought, which is not a remembrance of pleasure or pain; then what is the relationship between one who has that and another who has not? One has no image about another because the image is the movement of time, thought has built images step by step about another and that is no longer happening; but the other has made images about oneself step by step; for the other is in a movement of time and oneself has no time at all. One has this extraordinary sense of love which is not of time. What then is one's relationship with another? When one has that extraordinary quality of love then in that quality there is supreme intelligence. That intelligence is going to act in that relationship, it is not oneself who will act in that relationship. It is really a marvellous thing to go into because it totally alters all relationship; and if there is no such fundamental alteration in relationship there is no alteration in this monstrous society which we have built.

What is space? Can there be space without order? Just take an outward physical example: is there space when there is disorder in a room? When one throws one's clothes all over the place and everything is in disorder, is there space? There is only space when everything is in its right place. So, outwardly. Now inwardly: our minds are so confused, our whole life is self contradiction, disorder, caught in various habits, drugs, smoke, drink, sex and so on. Obviously habits are mechanical and where there are habits there is disorder. What is order inwardly? Is order something dictated by thought? Thought itself is a movement of disorder. One thinks one can bring about social order by very careful thought, by ideological thought. Society, whether in the West or the East, is in disorder, is confused, is contradictory and the world is so totally mad. Wherever there is the movement of thought, time-binding, fragmentary and limited in itself, there must be total disorder.

Is there an action which is not the result of the movement of thought; an action not conditioned by ideologies which have been put together by thought? Is there an action totally free from thought? Such action, then, would be complete, whole, total—not fragmentary, not contradictory. Such action would be whole action in which there is no regret, no sense of "I wish I hadn't done that", or "I will try to do that". Disorder comes about when there is the movement of thought and thought itself is fragmentary and when it acts everything must be fragmentary. If one sees that very clearly, then one asks: "What is action without thought?" Action means the doing now, not doing tomorrow, or having done in the past. It is as love, it is not of time. Love and compassion are beyond intellect, beyond memory; they are a state of mind that acts because love and compassion are supremely intelligent—intelligence acts. Where there is space, there is order, which is the action of intelligence; it is neither yours nor mine, it is intelligence born out of love and compassion. Space implies a mind that is not occupied; yet our minds are occupied all day long about something or other and so there is no space, not even an interval between two thoughts, every thought is associated with another thought so that there is no gap—the whole mind is crowded, chattering, with opinions and judgements.

True order brings enormous space; space means silence; out of silence comes this extraordinary sense of emptiness. Do not be frightened by that word "empty"; when there is emptiness then things can happen.

What is beauty? Does it lie in a picture, in a museum, in a poem? Does it lie in the line of the mountains against the sky; or in a sheet of water reflecting the beauty of the clouds, or in the line an architect gives a building; or in a home that has a certain beauty? What is beauty?—not the imagination that creates beauty; not the word that creates beauty; not a beautiful idea. When one sees something extraordinarily alive and beautiful, a mountain, a clear sky, a view, at that moment when seeing it totally one is absent, is one not? Because of the immensity of the mountain, its extraordinary stability, its sense of firmness and the line of it, its magnificence drives away the me—for the moment. The outer glory has driven away the petty little me—like a boy given a toy, he is absorbed by it, he will play with it for an hour and break it up and when you take the toy away he is back to himself, naughty, crying and mischievous. The same thing has happened; the great mountain has driven away the petty little me, and one sees it for the moment. When the me is absent, totally, there is beauty. Then one's relationship to nature changes completely; the earth becomes precious, every tree, every leaf, everything is part of that beauty—but man is destroying everything.

Is there anything sacred, holy? Obviously the things that thought has put together in the religious sense—investing sacredness in images, in ideas—are not sacred at all. That which is sacred has no division, not one a Christian, another a Hindu, Buddhist, Muslim and all the rest of the divisions. That which thought has put together is of time, is fragmentary, is not whole, therefore it is not holy, though you worship the image on a cross that is not holy, that is invested with sacredness by thought; the same with the images that the Hindus have put together, or the Buddhists and so on. What then is sacred? One can only find out when thought has discovered itself, its right place, without effort, without will and there is this immense sense of silence; the silence of the mind without any movement of thought. It is only when the mind is absolutely free and silent that one discovers that which is beyond all words, which is timeless. Then out of that comes the vastness of true meditation.

XV

When the me is not, then
compassion comes into being

No guru and no system can help one to understand oneself. Without understanding oneself there is no *raison d'être* to find out that which is right action, that which is truth. In investigating one's consciousness one is investigating the whole human consciousness—not only one's own—because one is the world and when one observes one's own consciousness one is observing the consciousness of mankind—it is not something personal and self-centred.

One of the factors in consciousness is desire. From perception, contact and sensation, thought creates the image and the pursuit of that image is the desire to fulfil, with all the frustration and the bitterness following from that. Now, can there be an observation of sensation not ending in desire? Just to observe. Which means one has to understand the nature of thought, because it is thought that gives continuity to desire; it is thought that creates the image out of sensation followed by the pursuit of that image.

Thought is the response of memory, experience and knowledge, stored up in the brain. Thought is never new, it is always from the past. Thought, therefore, is limited. Although it has created innumerable problems yet it has also created the extraordinary world of technology—marvellous things it has done. But thought is limited because it is the outcome of the past, therefore it is time-binding. Thought pretends to conceive the immeasurable, the timeless, something beyond itself; it projects all kinds of illusory images. Can one observe the whole movement of desire without images and the pursuit of those images; without thereby becoming involved in frustration, in the hope of fulfilment and so on? Just to observe the whole movement of desire; to become aware of it.

Can one psychologically be free yet not be caught up in the

198

illusion that one is free? That illusion comes about when one says to oneself: "I must be free from fear"—which is the movement of desire. Having understood the nature of desire and its movement, its images, its conflicts, then one can look at fear in oneself and not deceive oneself that one is psychologically free from fear. Then one can go into the whole question of fear; not a particular form of fear, but go to the very root of fear, which is much simpler and quicker than taking the various branches of fear and trimming them. By observing the totality of fear then come to the root of it. One can only go to the root of it when one observes the totality of the various forms of fears—observe, become aware of them, but not try to do something about them. By observing the whole tree of fear, with all the branches, with all its various qualities, all its divisions, go to the very root of it.

What is the root of fear, psychologically? Is not the root of fear, time?—what might happen tomorrow, or in the future; what might happen if one does not do certain things. Time as the past, time as what might happen now or in the future; is not the root of fear and time the movement of thought?

The root of fear is the movement of time; which is thought as measure. Can one observe, can one be aware of this movement, not controlling it, suppressing it, or escaping from it, but just observing it, being aware of its total movement? One is aware of this total movement of thought as time and measure—I have been, I shall be, I hope to be—one is choicelessly aware of this fact and remaining with it, not moving away from what actually is. What actually is, is the movement of thought, which says: "I have been hurt in the past and I hope I shall not be hurt in the future." That very process of thinking is fear—taking that as an example. Where there is fear, obviously there is no affection, there is no love.

A great part of consciousness is the enormous desire for and the pursuit of pleasure. All religions have said do not pursue pleasure, sexual or any kind of pleasure because you have given your life over to Jesus, or Krishna; they advocate suppressing desire, suppressing fear, suppressing any form of pleasure. Every religion has talked about it endlessly. We are saying: on the contrary do not suppress anything, do not avoid anything. Do not analyse one's fear—just observe. All human beings are caught in this pursuit of pleasure and when that pleasure is not given there is hatred, violence, anger and bitterness. So one must understand this pursuit, this enormous urge for pleasure which human beings have throughout the world.

The function of the brain is to register, as a computer registers. It registers pleasure, and thought gives the energy and the drive to pursue pleasure. One has had pleasure of various kinds yesterday: they are registered. Then thought says there must be more and thought then pursues the more. The more then becomes pleasure; the desire for continuity of pleasure is given vitality and driven by thought—thinking about it, today or tomorrow, later on. That is the movement of pleasure. Now: is it possible to register only that which is absolutely necessary and nothing else? We are continually registering so many things unnecessarily and so building up the self, the me—"I am hurt; I am not what I should be; I must achieve what I think should be", and so on. The whole of this registration is an action of giving importance to the self. Now we are asking: Is it possible to register only that which is absolutely necessary? What is absolutely necessary?—not all the things the psyche builds up, which are memories.

What is necessary to register and what is not necessary to register? The brain is occupied all the time with registering, therefore there is no tranquillity, no quietness, whereas if there is a clarity as to what is to be registered and what is not to be registered then the brain is quieter—and that is part of meditation.

Are the things that one registers psychologically necessary at all? Anything that you hold psychologically is unnecessary. By holding those things, registering those things, by the brain holding on to them, it attains a certain security; but that security is merely the me that has gathered all the psychological hurts and imprints. So we are saying: to register anything psychologically and hold it is absolutely unnecessary—one's beliefs, one's dogmas, one's experiences, one's wishes and desires, they are all totally unnecessary. So, what is it that is necessary? Food, clothes and shelter—nothing else. This is a tremendous thing to understand in oneself; it means that the brain is no longer the accumulating factor of the me. The brain is rested, tranquil and it needs considerable tranquillity; but it has always sought that tranquillity, that security, in the me which is the accumulation of all the past registrations, which are just memories, therefore worthless—like collecting a lot of dead ash and giving tremendous importance to it.

To register only that which is absolutely necessary; it is a marvellous thing if one can go into it and do it because then there is real freedom—freedom from all the accumulated knowledge, tradition, superstition and experience, which have all built up this enormous structure to which thought clings as the me. When the me is not, then compassion comes into being and that compassion brings clarity. With that clarity there is skill.

Where there is unnecessary registration there is no love. If one wants to understand the nature of compassion one has to go into this question of what love is and whether there is such a thing as love without any form of attachment with all its complications, with all its pleasures and fears.

XVI

The division between the
observer and the observed
is the source of conflict

There are two types of learning: one, memorizing what is being taught and then observing through memory—which is what most of us call learning—the other, learning through observation and not storing it as memory. Put another way: one is to learn something by heart, so that it is stored up in the brain as knowledge and subsequently acting according to that knowledge, skilfully or unskilfully; when one goes to school and university, one stores up a great deal of information as knowledge and according to that knowledge one acts, beneficially for oneself or for society; but incapable of acting simply, directly. The other kind of learning—to which one is not quite so accustomed because one is such a slave to habits, to tradition, to every form of conformity—is to observe without the accompaniment of previous knowledge, to look at something as though for the first time, afresh. If one observes things afresh, then there is not the cultivation of memory; it is not as when one observes and through that observation stores up memory so that the next time one observes it is through that pattern of memory, therefore not anymore observing afresh.

It is important to have a mind that is not constantly occupied, constantly chattering. To an unoccupied mind a new seed of learning can germinate—something entirely different from the cultivation of knowledge and acting from that knowledge.

Observe the skies, the beauty of the mountains, the trees, the light among the leaves. That observation, if stored up as memory, will prevent the next observation being fresh. When one observes one's wife or friend, can one observe without the interference of the recording of previous incidents in that particular relationship? If one can observe or watch the other without the interference of previous knowledge, one learns much more.

The most important thing is to observe; to observe and not to have a division between the observer and the observed. Mostly there is a division as between the observer who is the total summation of past experience as memory and the observed, that which is—so the past observes. The division between the observer and the observed is the source of conflict.

Is it possible for there to be no conflict at all, right through one's life? Traditionally, one accepts that there must be this conflict, this struggle, this everlasting fight, not only physiologically in order to survive, but psychologically in desire and fear, like and dislike, and so on. To live without conflict is to live a life without any effort, a life in which there is peace. Man has lived, centuries upon centuries, a life of battle, conflict, both outwardly and inwardly; a constant struggle to achieve and fear of losing, dropping back. One may talk endlessly about peace, but there will be no peace as long as one is conditioned to the acceptance of conflict. If one says it is possible to live in peace, then it is just an idea and therefore valueless. And if one says it is not possible, then one blocks any investigation.

Go into it psychologically first; it is more important than physiologically. If one understands very deeply the nature and the structure of conflict psychologically and perhaps ends it there, then one may be able to deal with the physiological factor. But if one is only concerned with the physiological, biological factor, to survive, then one probably will not be able to do it at all.

Why is there this conflict, psychologically? From ancient times, both socially and religiously, there has been a division between the good and the bad. Is there really this division at all—or is there only "what is", without its opposite? Suppose there is anger; that is the fact, that is "what is", but "I will not be angry" is an idea, not a fact.

One never questions this division, one accepts it because one is traditional by habit, not wanting anything new. But there is a further factor; there is a division between the observer and the observed. When one looks at a mountain, one looks at it as an observer and one calls it a mountain. The word is not the thing. The word "mountain" is not the mountain, but to oneself the word is very important; when one looks, instantly there is the response, "that is a mountain". Now, can one look at the thing called "mountain", without the word, because the word is a factor of division? When one says "My wife," the word "my" creates division. The word, the name, is part of thought. When one looks at a man or a woman, a mountain or a tree, whatever it is, division takes place when thought, the name, the memory, comes into being.

Can one observe without the observer, who is the essence of all the memories, experiences, reactions and so on, which are from the past? If one looks at something without the word and the past memories, then one looks without the observer. When one does that, there is only the observed and there is no division and no conflict, psychologically. Can one look at one's wife or one's nearest intimate friend without the name, the word and all the experiences that one has gathered in that relationship? When one so looks one is looking at her or him for the first time.

Is it possible to live a life that is completely free from all psychological conflict? One has observed the fact, it will do everything if one lets the fact alone. As long as there is division between the image-making observer, and the fact—which is no image but only fact—there must be everlasting conflict. That is a law. That conflict can be ended.

When there is an ending of psychological conflict—which is part of suffering—then how does that apply to one's livelihood, how does that apply in one's relationship with others? How does that ending of psychological struggle, with all its conflicts, pain, anxiety, fear, how does that apply to one's daily living—one's daily going to the office etc. etc.? If it is a fact that one has ended psychological conflict, then how will one live a life without conflict outwardly? When there is no conflict inside, there is no conflict outside, because there is no division between the inner and the outer. It is like the ebb and flow of the sea. It is an absolute, irrevocable fact, which nobody can touch, it is inviolate. So, if that is so, then what shall one do to earn a livelihood? Because there is no conflict, therefore there is no ambition. Because there is no conflict, there is no desire to be something. Because inwardly there is something absolute which is inviolate, which cannot be touched, which cannot be damaged, then one does not depend psychologically on another; therefore there is no conformity, no imitation. So, not having all that, one is no longer heavily conditioned to success and failure in the world of money, position, prestige, which implies the denial of "what is" and the acceptance of "what should be".

Because one denies "what is" and creates the ideal of "what should be" there is conflict. But to observe what actually is, means one has no opposite, only "what is". If you observe violence and use the word "violence" there is already conflict, the very word is already warped: there are people who approve of violence and people who do not. The whole philosophy of non-violence is warped, both politically and religiously. There is violence and its opposite, non-violence. The opposite exists because you know violence. The opposite has its root in violence. One thinks that by having an opposite, by some extraordinary method or means, one will get rid of "what is".

Now, can one put away the opposite and just look at violence, the fact? The non-violence is not a fact. Non-violence is an idea, a concept, a conclusion. The fact is violence—that one is angry; that one hates somebody; that one wants to hurt people; that one is jealous; all that is the implication of violence, that is the fact. Now, can one observe that fact without introducing its opposite? For then one has the energy—which was being wasted in trying to achieve the opposite—to observe "what is". In that observation there is no conflict.

So, what will a man do who has understood this extraordinary complex existence based on violence, conflict, struggle, a man who is actually free of it, not theoretically, but actually free? Which means, no conflict. What shall he do in the world? Will one ask this question if one is inwardly, psychologically, completely free from conflict? Obviously not. It is only the man in conflict who says: "If there is no conflict, I will be at an end, I will be destroyed by society because society is based on conflict."

If one is aware of one's consciousness, what is one? If one is aware, one will see that one's consciousness is—in its absolute sense—in total disorder. It is contradictory, saying one thing, doing something else, always wanting something. The total movement is within an area which is confined and without space and in that little space there is disorder.

Is one different from one's consciousness? Or is one that consciousness? One is that consciousness. Then is one aware that one is in total disorder? Ultimately that disorder leads to neurosis, obviously—and all the specialists in modern society such as psychoanalysts, psychotherapists and so on. But inwardly, is one in order? Or is there disorder? Can one observe this fact? And what takes place when one observes choicelessly—which means without any distortion? Where there is disorder, there must be conflict. Where there is absolute order there is no conflict. And there is an absolute order, not relative order. That can only come about naturally, easily, without any conflict, when one is aware of oneself as a consciousness, aware of the confusion, the turmoil, the contradiction, outwardly and inwardly observing without any distortion. Then out of that comes naturally, sweetly, easily, an order which is irrevocable.

XVII

When there is an ending
to consciousness with its content
there is something entirely different

To observe holistically is to observe—or to listen to—the whole content of something. Normally, we look at things partially, according to our pleasure, or according to our conditioning, or according to some idealistic point of view; we always look at things fragmentarily. The politician is mostly concerned with politics; the economist, the scientist, the business man, each has his own concern, generally throughout life. It seems that we never take, or observe, the whole movement of life—like a full river with a great volume of water behind it; water right from beginning to end. It may become polluted but, given sufficient extent, it can cleanse itself. So, in the same way, we can treat life holistically, moving totally from the beginning to the end without any fragmentation, without any deviation, without any illusion. It is important to understand how the mind creates illusions of self-importance and all the various types of illusions which are comforting and safe—at least for the time being. We look at something with a preconceived idea or belief, so that we never really actually see it.

Illusions are created by seeking satisfaction in desire. Satisfaction is entirely different from ecstacy. Ecstacy is a state of being, or not being, which is outside of oneself. That is ecstacy in which there is no experiencing. The moment there is experiencing, then it is the self with its past memories, its recollections, which is translating, creating illusions. Ecstacy never creates illusions. You cannot hold on to ecstacy because it is outside of oneself; there is no question of remembering it; there is no question of wanting it; wanting it is the desire to satisfy and that creates illusion.

Most of us are caught in some kind of illusion—the illusion of being, or not being, the illusion of power, position and so on: whole categories projected from the centre, which is the me. Illusion means to see sensuously through a definite conclusion, prejudice, or idea.

A mind that is caught in illusions has no order. Order can only come about holistically. We need order; even in a very small room one puts things in their right place otherwise it becomes disorderly, ugly, and lacking repose. We think order, psychologically, is in the following of a certain pattern or a certain routine which we have already established in the past. Order is, psychologically, something entirely different; it can only come about when there is clarity. Clarity brings order, not the other way round; try to seek order then that becomes mechanistic, a conformity to a pattern in which there can be no clarity.

Order implies harmony in daily life. Harmony is not an idea. We are caught in the prison of ideas and there is no harmony in that. Harmony and clarity imply seeing things holistically, observing life as a total unitary movement—not, I am a business man at the office and a different person at home; not, I am an artist and can do the most absurd and eccentric things; not this breaking up, or fragmenting, of life into various categories, the élite and the non-élite, the worker and the non-worker, the intellectual and the romantic, which is the way we normally live. See how important it is to treat life as a total movement in which everything is included, in which there is no breaking down, as the good and the bad and heaven and hell. See holistically so that when you observe your friend, or your wife or your husband, you see holistically in that relationship.

We think of freedom as freedom from something—freedom from sorrow, from anxiety, from work—which is really reaction and therefore not freedom at all. When someone says "I am free from smoking", that is a response from what has been, a moving away from what has been. But we are talking of freedom which is not *from* something, which implies observing holistically.

In observing holistically there is no fragmentation, or direction in that observation; for when there is direction there is distortion. Only when there is complete freedom can you observe holistically and in that observation there is no satisfaction and therefore there is no illusion.

So, observe life as a total movement, non-fragmented, holistic, flowing continuously—"continuously" but not in the sense of time. Usually the word "continuous" implies time; but there is a continuity which is not of time. We think of the relationship between the past and the future as a continuity, without breaking up. That is what we generally understand by the word "continuity", which is of time. Time is movement, a time-span to be covered through days, months, or years, with an ideal to be achieved at the end of it. Time implies thought; thought is a movement of measure; the movement of time. But, is there a continuity—if we can use that word, which is not perhaps quite right—is there a continuity which is not a series of incidents related to the past as cause becoming effect now and the effect in turn becoming future cause? Is there a state of being in which there is an ending, a coming to an end, of everything?

We think of life as a measured movement in time; a movement which ends in death. Up to that point that is what we call continuity. Yet one observes a movement which is not of time, which is not a remembrance of something of the past going through the present and modifying the future and so continuing. There is a state of mind which is dying to everything that is happening; all that happens is coming in and flowing out—there is no retaining, but always a flowing out. That state of mind has its own sense of beauty and "continuity" which is not of time.

Every religion, from ancient times, has tried to find out if there is something beyond death. The Ancient Egyptians thought that, in a way, living is part of death, so you carried over your slaves, your cattle, as you died. To go over to the other side was to live as you have lived this side, in the past. That was a continuity. The ancient people of India said life must have a continuity; for otherwise what is the point of achieving moral character, having so much experience in life, having suffered so much, if it merely ends in death—what is the point of it? Therefore, they said, there must be a future and in that future the content of consciousness is modified life after life; its content went on. The Christians have a different kind of fulfilment, such as the resurrection and so on. But, we want to find the truth of it; not what you think, not what the professionals, the priests and the psychologists think. There have appeared certain articles in the press in America and Europe affirming that people have "died" and come back to daily life remembering having experienced extraordinary "after death" states, light, beauty—whatever. One questions whether they really died, because if one is really dead it means that oxygen is not going to the brain and after several minutes the brain deteriorates; when there is real death there is no coming back and therefore no recollection of something after you die. Death may be a most extraordinary experience, much greater than so-called love, much greater than any desire, any idea, any conclusion; or it may be the end of everything, of every form of relationship, every form of recollection, remembrance, accumulation. It may be total annihilation; the complete ending of everything. One must find out what is the truth of the matter.

To come upon the truth, every form of identification must end, every form of fear, every desire for comfort. One must not be caught in that illusion which says: "Yes, there is a marvellous state after death." The mind must have no identification with the name, with the form, or with any person, idea, conclusion. Is that possible? That does not deny love; on the contrary, when one is attached to a person there is no love; there is dependence; there is the fear of being left alone in a world where everything is so insecure, both psychologically and outwardly. To find out what is the truth of death, what is the meaning, the real depth, of that extraordinary thing that must happen, there must be freedom. And there is no freedom when there is attachment, when there is fear, when there is a desire for comfort. Can one put all that aside? To find the truth of this extraordinary thing called death one must also find the truth of what is before death; not the truth after death, but also the truth before death. What is the truth before death? If that is not clear the other cannot be clear. One must look very closely, carefully and freely, at what is before death, which we call living. What is the truth of one's living?—which means what is one, or who is one—which one calls living? A heavily conditioned mind brought about through education, environment, culture, through religious sanctions, beliefs and dogmas, rituals, "my country", "your country", the constant battle, wanting to be happy and being unhappy, depressed and elated, going through anxiety, uncertainty, hate, envy and the pursuit of pleasure; afraid to be alone, fear of loneliness, old age, disease—this is the truth of our life, our daily life. Can such a mind, which has not put order in this life—order in the sense of that which comes through clarity and compassion—can such a mind which is so utterly fragmented, disorderly, frightened, find out the truth about something outside of all that?

So what is the truth of death—that is, complete ending? There may be annihilation, or there may be something; but that is a hope creating distortion and illusion; so one is cutting that out.

One can only find out the truth of it when there is an ending—an ending to everything that you have; the ending to attachment, not giving it a day, ending it completely, now. That is what death means—ending, complete ending; and when there is complete ending something new is born.

Fear is a burden, a terrible burden and when one removes that burden completely there is something new that takes place. But one is afraid of ending—either ending at the end of one's life, or ending now. End your vanity, because without ending there is no beginning. We are caught in this continuity of never ending. When there is total, complete, holistic, ending there is something totally new beginning, which you cannot possibly imagine; it is a totally different dimension.

To find out the truth of death, there must be the ending of the content of one's consciousness. Then one will never ask "Who am I?" or "What am I?" One is one's consciousness with its content. When there is an ending to that consciousness with its content there is something entirely different, which is not imagined. Human beings have sought immortality in their actions; one writes a book and in that book there is one's immortality as a writer; a great painter makes a painting and that painting becomes the immortality of that human being. All that must end—which no artist is willing to do.

Each human being is a representative of the whole of humanity and when there is that change in consciousness one brings about a change in the human consciousness. Death is the ending of this consciousness as one knows it.

XVIII

Without clarity, skill becomes a most dangerous thing

When one has developed a skill it gives a certain sense of well-being, security. And that skill, born of knowledge, must invariably, in its action, become mechanical. Skill in action is what one has sought because it gives a certain position in society, a certain prestige. Living in that field all the time, as one does in modern society, with all its economic demands, that knowledge and skill become, not only additive but also invariably a repetitive mechanical process that gradually gathers its own stimulation, its own arrogance, and power. In that power one has security.

Society, at the present time, is demanding more and more skill—whether one is an engineer, a technological expert, a scientist, a psycho-therapist, etc. etc.—but there is great danger—is there not?—is seeking all this skill resulting from accumulated knowledge, for in this increase there is no clarity. When skill becomes all important in life, not only because it is the means of livelihood, but because one is totally educated for that purpose—all our schools, colleges and universities are directed for that purpose—then that skill invariably brings about a certain sense of power, of arrogance and self-importance.

The art of learning is not only in the accumulation of the knowledge necessary for skilful action, but also in that learning which is without accumulation. There are two types of learning: acquiring and accumulating a great deal of knowledge through experience, through books, through education which may be used in skilful action; and another form in which one never accumulates and in which one never registers anything other than that which is absolutely necessary. In the first form, the brain is registering and accumulating knowledge, storing it up and acting from that store skilfully, or unskilfully. In the second form, one becomes so totally aware that one only registers that which is absolutely necessary and nothing else; then the mind is not cluttered and influenced with the movement of accumulated knowledge.

In this art of learning, accumulating knowledge, by registering only the things that are necessary for skilful action, there is the non-registering of any psychological reactions; the brain is employing knowledge where function and skill are necessary and yet the brain is free not to register in the psychological area. It is very arduous this, to be so totally aware that one only registers that which is necessary and not, absolutely does not, register anything which is unnecessary. Someone insults you, someone flatters you, someone calls you this or that—no registration. This gives tremendous clarity. To register and yet not to register so that there is no psychological building up of the me, the structure of the self. The structure of the self arises only when there is the registration of everything that is not necessary; that is: giving importance to one's name, one's experience, one's opinions and conclusions, all that is the intensifying of the energy in the self—which is always distorting.

The art of learning gives this extraordinary clarity and if there is great skill in action without that clarity then it breeds self-importance, whether the self-importance is identified with oneself or with a group, or with a nation. Self-importance denies clarity. There cannot be compassion without clarity and because there is no compassion skill has become so important. If there is no clarity there is no awakening of intelligence, that intelligence which is neither yours nor mine, it is intelligence. That intelligence has its own action, which is non-mechanistic and therefore without cause.

As in the art of seeing and of listening, in the art of learning there is no movement of thought. Thought is necessary to accumulate knowledge to function skilfully, otherwise thought has no place whatsoever. This brings tremendous clarity. In such clarity there is no centre from which one is functioning; no centre which has been put together by thought, as the me, mine; for where there is that centre there must be a circumference, where there is a circumference there is resistance, there is the division which is one of the fundamental causes of fear. Without clarity skill becomes a most destructive thing in life—which is what is happening in the world; men can go to the moon and put the flag of their country there, but that is not from clarity; they can kill each other through wars as a result of the extraordinary development of technology, all from the movement of thought, which is not clarity. Thought can never understand that which is whole, that which is immeasurable, which is timeless.

XIX

How is one to know oneself?

What is the nature of thought that it ceases when there is complete attention and when there is no attention it arises? One has to understand what it is to be aware otherwise one will not be able to understand completely the full significance of attention.

Is there an idea of awareness or is one aware? There is a difference. The *idea* of being aware, or *being* aware. "Aware" means to be sensitive, to be alive, to the things about one, to nature, to people, to colour, to the trees, to the environment, to the social structure, the whole thing, to be aware outwardly of all that is happening and to be aware to what is happening inside. To be aware is to be sensitive, to know, to observe, what is happening inside psychologically and also what is happening outside, environmentally, economically, socially and so on. If one is not aware of what is happening outwardly and one begins to be aware inwardly then one becomes rather neurotic. But if one begins to be aware of what is exactly happening in the world, as much as possible, and then from there moves inwardly, then one has a balance. Then there is a possibility of not deceiving oneself. One begins by being aware of what is happening outwardly and then one moves inward—like the ebb and flow of the tide, there is constant movement—so that there is no deception. If one knows what is happening outside and from there moves inward one then has criteria.

How is one to know oneself? Oneself is a very complex structure, a very complex movement; how is one to know oneself so that one does not deceive oneself? One can only know oneself in one's relationship to others. In one's relationship to others one may withdraw from them because one does not want to be hurt and in relationship one may discover that one is very jealous, dependent, attached and really quite callous. So relationship acts as a mirror in which one knows oneself. It is the same thing outwardly; the outer is a reflection of oneself, because society, governments, all these things, are created by human beings fundamentally the same as oneself.

To find out what awareness is one must go into the question of order and disorder. One sees outwardly that there is a great deal of disorder, confusion and uncertainty. What has brought about this uncertainty, this disorder; who is responsible? Are we? Be quite clear as to whether we are responsible for the disorder outwardly; or is it some divine disorder out of which divine order will come? So, if one feels responsible for the outward disorder then is not that disorder an expression of one's own disorder?

One observes that disorder outwardly is created by our disorder inwardly. As long as human beings have no order in themselves there will be disorder, always. Governments may try to control that disorder, outwardly; the extreme form is the totalitarianism of Marxism—saying it knows what order is, you do not, it is going to tell you what it is and suppress you, or confine you in concentration camps and psychiatric hospitals and all that follows.

The world is in disorder because we are in disorder, each one of us. Is one *aware* of one's disorder or has one but a *concept* of disorder? Is one aware that one is in disorder or is it merely an idea which has been suggested that one accepts? The acceptance of an idea is an abstraction, an abstraction from "what is". The abstraction is to move away from "what is"—and one mostly lives in ideas and moves away from facts. Is one accepting a concept of disorder or is one aware that one is oneself in disorder? Does one understand the difference between the two? Does one become aware, *per se*, for itself?

What does one mean by disorder? There is contradiction; one thinks one thing, and does another. There is the contradiction of opposing desires, opposing demands, opposing movements in oneself—duality. How does this duality arise? Is it not that one is incapable of looking at "what is"? One would rather run away from "what is" into "what should be", hoping somehow, by some miracle, by some effort of will, to change "what is" into "what should be". That is: one is angry and one "should not" be angry. If one knew what to do with anger, how to deal with anger and go beyond it, there would be no need for "what should be", which is "do not be angry". If one can understand what to do with "what is", then one will not escape to "what should be". Because one does not know what to do with "what is", one hopes that by inventing an ideal that one can somehow through the ideal change "what is". Or, because one is incapable and does not know what to do, one's brain becomes conditioned to living always in the future—the "what one hopes to be". One is essentially living in the past but one hopes by living for an ideal in the future to alter the present. If one were to see what to do with "what is" then the future does not matter. It is not a question of accepting "what is", but remaining with "what is".

One can only understand something if one looks at "what is" and does not run away from it—not try to change it into something else. Can one remain with, observe, see, "what is"—nothing else? I want to look at "what is". I realize that I am greedy but it does not do anything. Greed is a feeling and I have looked at that feeling named greed. The word is not the thing; but I may be mistaking the word for the thing. I may be caught in words but not with the fact—the fact that I am greedy. It is very complex; the word may incite that feeling. Can the mind be free of the word and look? The word has become so important to me in my life. Am I a slave to words?—knowing that the word is not the thing. Has the word become so important that the fact is not real, actual, to me? I would rather look at a picture of a mountain than go and look at a mountain; to look at a mountain I have to go a great distance, climb, look, feel. Looking at a picture of a mountain is looking at a symbol, it is not reality. Am I caught in words, which are symbols, thereby moving away from reality? Does the word create the feeling of greed?—or is there greed without the word? This requires tremendous discipline, not suppression. The very pursuit of the enquiry has its own discipline. So I have to find out, very carefully, whether the word has created the feeling, or if the feeling exists without the word. The word is greed, I named it when I had that feeling before therefore I am registering the present feeling by a past incident of the same kind. So the present has been absorbed into the past.

So I realize what I am doing. I am aware that the word has become extraordinarily important to me. So then, is there a freedom from the word greed, envy or nationality, Communist, Socialist and so on—is there a freedom from the word? The word is of the past. The feeling is the present recognized by the word from the past, so I am living all the time in the past. The past is me. The past is time; so time is me. The me says: "I must not be angry because my conditioning has said: do not be greedy, do not be angry." The past is telling the present what it should do. So there is a contradiction because fundamentally, very deeply, the past is dictating the present, what it should do. The me, which is the past with all its memories, experiences, knowledge, a thing put together by thought, the me, is dictating what should happen.

Now, can I observe the fact of greed without the past? Can there be observation of greed without naming, without getting caught in the word, having understood that the word can create the feeling and that if the word creates the feeling then the word is 'me', which is of the past, telling me "do not be greedy"? Is it possible to look at "what is" without the me—which is the observer? Can I observe greed, the feeling, its fulfilment and action, without the observer which is the past?

The "what is" can only be observed when there is no me. Can one observe the colours and forms around one? How does one observe them? One observes through the eye. Observe without moving the eye; because if one moves the eye the whole operation of the thinking brain comes into being. The moment the brain is in operation there is distortion. Look at something without moving one's eyes; how still the brain becomes. Observe not only with one's eyes but with all one's care, with affection. There is then an observation of the fact, not the idea, but the fact, with care and with affection. One approaches "what is" with care, with affection; therefore there is no judgement, no condemnation; therefore one is free of the opposite.

PART III

Krishnamurti talks with a small group at Ojai drawn from the Krishnamurti Schools and Foundations in Canada, England, India and USA

I

Questioner (1): Can we discuss the relation between Krishnamurti's teaching and truth?

Questioner (2): Is there such a thing as a teaching at all, or is there only truth?

KRISHNAMURTI: Is it the expression of truth? There are two things involved. The speaker is either talking out of the silence of truth, or he is talking out of the noise of an illusion which he considers to be the truth.

Q: That is what most people do.

K: So which is it that he is doing?

Q: There could be a confusion between the word and truth.

K: No, the word is not the truth. That's why we said: either he is talking out of the silence of truth or out of the noise of illusion.

Q: But because one feels that he is speaking out of the silence of truth there is a greater possibility for the word to be taken as truth.

K: No, let's go slowly for this is interesting. Who is going to judge, who is going to see the truth of the matter? The listener, the reader? You who know Indian scriptures, Buddhism, *The Upanishads*, etc.—you are familiar with them and know most of the contents of all that. Are you capable of judging? How shall we find out? You hear him talking about these things and you wonder if he is really speaking out of this extraordinary silence of truth, or as a reaction and from a conditioned childhood and so on. That is to say, either he is talking out of his conditioning or out of the other. How will you find out? How will you approach this problem?

Q: Is it possible for me to find out if what is meeting that teaching is the noise within myself?

K: That's why I am asking you. What is the criterion, the measure that you apply so you can say: "Yes, that is it." Or do you say: "I don't know"? I am asking what you do. Or don't you know but are examining, investigating; not whether he is speaking out of silence

221

or conditioning, but you are watching the truth of what he is saying. I would want to know whether he was speaking out of this, or out of that. But as I don't know, I am going to listen to what he is saying and see if it is true.

Q: But what sees it as true?

K: Say one is fairly alive to things. One listens to this man and one wants to find out whether what he says is mere words or the truth.

Q: When I have come to the conclusion that it is the truth, then I am already not listening.

K: No, I don't know. My life is concerned with this problem—not just for a few years or a few days. I want to know the truth of this matter. Is he speaking out of experience or from knowledge, or not out of any of these things? Most people speak out of knowledge, so we are asking that question.

I don't know how *you* would find out. I'll tell you what I would do. I would put his personality, his influence, all that, completely aside. Because I don't want to be influenced, I am sceptical, doubtful, so I am very careful. I listen to him and I don't say "I know" or "I don't know", but I am sceptical. I want to find out.

Q: Sceptical means you are inclined to doubt it, which is already a bias . . .

K: Oh, no! I am sceptical in the sense that I don't accept everything that is being said.

Q: But you lean towards doubting. It's negation.

K: Oh, no. I would rather use the word doubt, in the sense of questioning. Let's put it that way. I say to myself: Am I questioning out of my prejudice? This question has never been put to me before, I am exploring it. I would put everything aside—all the personal reputation, charm, looks, this and that—I am not going to accept or reject, I am going to listen to find out. Am I prejudiced? Am I listening to him with all the knowledge I have gathered about religion, of what the books have said, what other people have said, or what my own experience tells me?

Q: No. I may be listening to him precisely because I have rejected all that.

K: Have I rejected it? Or am I listening to him with all that? If I have rejected that then I am listening. Then I am listening very carefully to what he has to say.

Q: Or I am listening with everything that I already know of him?

K: I have said: I have put away his reputation. Am I listening to him with the knowledge that I have acquired through books, through experience, and therefore I am comparing, judging, evaluating? Then I can't find out whether what he is saying is the truth. But is it possible for me to put aside all that? I am passionately interested to find out. So for the time being—while I am listening at least—I will put aside everything I have known. Then I proceed. I want to know, but I am not going to be easily persuaded, pulled into something by argument, cleverness, logic. Now am I capable of listening to what he is saying with complete abandonment of the past? It comes to that. Are you? Then my relationship to him is entirely different. Then I am listening out of silence.

This is really a very interesting question. I have answered for myself. There are a dozen of us here, how would *you* answer it? How do you *know* that what he is talking about is the truth?

Q: I wouldn't be concerned with that word truth. When you use the word truth you indicate you have the ability to judge what is true, or you already have a definition of truth, or you know what truth is. Which means you will not be listening to what somebody is saying.

K: Don't you want to know whether he is speaking falsehood, out of a conditioned mind, from a rejection and therefore out of a reaction?

Q (1): I realize that in order to listen to this man I can't listen with a conditioned mind—*not to anybody*.

Q (2): Another question which arises is: I reject all this knowledge and listen in silence. Is truth in that silence?

K: I don't know. That is one of the things I have got to find out.

Q (1): If there is no rejection there is no silence.

Q (2): As this well is an endless source, is the teaching the same as truth?

K: How would you answer this question?

Q: I think first of all you can be sensitive to what is false. In other words, to see if there is something false, something incoherent.

K: Logic can be very false.

223

Q (1): Yes, I don't mean just logic, but you can be sensitive to the whole communication to see if there is some deception. I think one of the questions implied here is: Are you deceiving yourself?

Q (2): But doesn't that sensitivity imply the absence of one's own projections—the silence after having moved through all your own colouring of it. Only then can you be that sensitive.

Q (3): You have to be free of deceiving yourself to see that.

K: Again, forgive me for asking: How do you know he is speaking the truth? Or is he deceiving himself and is caught in an illusion which gives him a feeling that he is telling the truth? What do you answer?

Q: One goes into it oneself. One cannot accept it without going deeply into it.

K: But one can deceive oneself so appallingly.

Q: You go through the layers of all those deceptions and beyond them.

K: If I were a stranger I might say: You have listened to this man for a long time, how do you know he is telling the truth? How do you know anything about it?

Q: I could say that I have looked at what you have said, and each time I was able to test it to see if it was right. I have not found anything which was contradictory.

K: No. The question was: How do you find out the truth?—Not about contradiction, logic, all that. One's own sensitivity, one's own investigation, one's own delving—is that enough?

Q (1): If one goes all the way, if one goes through all the possible self-deceptions.

Q (2): And then goes so far as to say that in the moments when one is listening—I do not know how deeply, but listening at all—one feels there is a change in oneself. It may not be a total revolution, but there is a change.

K: That can happen when you go for a walk and look at the mountains and are quiet, and when you come back to your home certain things have taken place. You follow what I am saying?

Q (1): Yes.

Q (2): We listen to people who speak from knowledge, and we listen to you, and there is something totally different. The non-verbal . . .

K: Have you answered the question?

Q (1): To myself I have. I have listened to scores of people and I listen to K. I don't know what it is, but it is totally different.

Q (2): That means there is a ring of truth in it.

Q (3): There are people who imply that in some way you are deceiving yourself. They do not see it that way.

Q (4): There was a man who wrote to me and asked if I agreed with everything Krishnamurti said. "Didn't he tell you that you should doubt everything he said?" The only way I could answer was to say: "Look, to me it is self evident."

K: It may be self evident to you and yet an illusion. It is such a dangerous, delicate thing.

Q (1): It can be that there is a scale on which we weigh it.

Q (2): I think that for thought it is not at all possible to be sure about this matter. It is typical of thought that it wants to be sure that it is not deceiving itself, that it is listening to truth. Thought will never give up that question, and it is right for thought never to give up questioning, but thought cannot touch it, cannot know about it.

K: Dr Bohm and I had a discussion of this kind in a different way. If I remember rightly we said: Is there such a silence which is not the word, which is not imagined or induced? Is there such a silence, and is it possible to speak out of that silence?

Q: The question was whether the words are coming from perception, from the silence, or from the memory.

K: Yes.

Q: The question is whether the words that are used are communicating directly and are coming out of the emptiness, out of the silence, or not.

K: That is the real question.

Q: As we used to say: like the drum which vibrates to the emptiness within.

K: Yes. Are you satisfied by this answer?—by what the others have said?

Q: No, Krishnaji.

K: Then how do you find out?

Q: The very words you are using deny the possibility of being satisfied and to work at it intellectually. It is something that has nothing to do with those things.

K: Look, suppose I love you and trust you. Because I trust you and you trust me whatever you say won't be a lie and I know you won't deceive me under any circumstances, you won't tell me something which is not actual to you.

Q: I might do something out of ignorance.

K: But say you trust me and I trust you. There is a relationship of trust, confidence, affection, love; like a man and a woman when they are married, they trust each other. Now is that possible here? Because—as she points out—I can deceive myself with logic, with reason, with all these things: millions of people have done it. I can also see the danger of, "I love the priest"; and he can play havoc with me.

Q (1): If one has affection for someone, one projects all kinds of illusions on to him.

Q (2): I think the trust, the investigation, logic and all that goes together with love.

K: That is a very dangerous thing too.

Q (1): Of course it is.

Q (2): Isn't there any way to avoid danger?

K: I don't want to be caught in an illusion.

Q: So can we say that truth is in the silence out of which the teaching comes?

K: But I want to know how the silence comes! I might invent it. I might have worked to have a silent mind for years, conditioned it, kept it in a cage, and then say, "Marvellous, I am silent". There is that danger. Logic is a danger. Thought is a danger. So I see all the dangers around me. I am caught in all these dangers and I want to find out if what that man is saying is the truth.

Q (1): I think there is no way or procedure to find that out. There is no prescription. I cannot tell anybody how to find out. I can say that I feel it with all my being, that something is true and maybe I can convey it through my life, but I cannot convince anybody through words or reason or by any method. And in the same way I cannot convince myself.

Q (2): Are we saying that perception has to be pure and in the realm of silence—the real realm of silence, not a fantasy—in order to be able to even come close to this question?

K: Dr Bohm is a scientist, a physicist, he is clear-thinking, logical; suppose someone goes to him and asks, "Is what Krishnamurti says the truth?" How is he going to answer?

Q: Doesn't Dr Bohm, or anybody, have to go beyond the limitations of logic?

K: Somebody comes to him and asks: "Tell me, I really want to know from you, please tell me if that man is speaking the truth."

Q: But you are then saying, use the instrument of logic to find out?

K: No. I am very interested because I have heard so many people who are illogical and careless say he is speaking the truth. But I go to a serious thinker, careful with the use of words, and ask: "Please tell me if he is telling the truth, not some crooked thing covered up." How is he going to answer me?

Q: The other day when that man said you may be caught in a groove,* and you looked at it first, what happened then?

K: I looked at it in several different ways and I don't think I am caught in a groove, but yet I might be. So after examining it very carefully, I left it. Something takes place when you leave it alone after an examination, something new comes into it.

Now I am asking you: Please tell me if that man is speaking the truth.

Q: For me it is a reality. I can't communicate it to you. This is what I have found out and you have to find it out for yourself. You have to test it in your own mind.

K: But you may be leading me up the garden path.

Q: That is all I can say. I can't really communicate it.

K: You may be up the garden path yourself.

Q (1): But then why should I go to Dr Bohm, much as I respect him?

* See Dialogue II, pages 234–5 and 236–7.

Q (2): One thing I can say is that I have questioned it and I have said it may be so, it may not be so, and I have looked carefully into the question of self-deception.

Q (3): It seems to me I would want to know what he is bringing to bear on the answer to this question. Is it science? Is it logic? Is it his own intelligence? I would want to know out of what he was going to answer me.

K: How do you in your heart of hearts, as a human being, know that he is speaking the truth? I want to *feel* it. I object to logic and all that. I have been through that before. Therefore if all that is not the way, then what is?

Q: There are people who are very clever, who speak of things which are very similar, who have grasped this intellectually very well and say they are speaking from truth.

K: Yes, they are repeating in India now: "You are the world." That is the latest catch-word!

Q: In order to communicate that, I have to speak out of the silence you were referring to.

K: No, please be simple with me. I want to know if Krishnamurti is speaking the truth. Dr Bohm has known Krishnamurti for several years. He has a good, trained mind so I go to him and ask him.

Q: All he can say is, "I know this man, this is how he affects me. He has changed my life." And suddenly a note may be struck in the other one.

K: No. I want it straight from the horse's mouth!

Q (1): Dr Bohm is here. Let him tell us.

Q (2): But you said you wanted proof.

K: I don't. It is a very serious question, it isn't just a dramatic or intellectual question. This is a tremendous question.

Q: Can one ever get an answer? Or is that person asking a false question to begin with?

K: Is he?

Q (1): Of course. How can a person know?

Q (2): I think I could say to him that when we did discuss these things it was from the emptiness, and that I felt it was a direct perception.

K: Yes. Is direct perception unrelated to logic?

Q: It doesn't come from logic.

K: But you are logical all the same.

Q: That may come later, not at that moment.

K: So you are telling me: I have found out that man is telling the truth because I had a direct perception, an insight into what he is saying.

Q: Yes.

K: Now be careful, because I have heard a disciple of some guru saying exactly the same thing.

Q: I have also heard a guru say this but a little later by looking at it logically I saw the thing was nonsense. When I was looking at the fact and the logic I saw that it did not fit. So I would say that in addition to direct perception I have constantly examined this logically.

K: So you are saying that perception has not blinded you and with that perception goes logic also.

Q: Yes, logic and fact.

K: So perception first, then logic. Not first logic, then perception.

Q: Yes. That is what it always has to be.

K: So through perception and then with logic, you see that it is the truth. Hasn't this been done by the devout Christians?

Q: Logic is not enough, because we have to see how people actually behave as well. I see that Christians say certain things, but when we look at the whole of what they do it doesn't fit.

K: Isn't there a terrible danger in this?

Q: I am sure there is a danger.

K: So you are now saying that one has to walk in danger.

Q: Yes.

K: Now I begin to understand what you are saying. One has to move in a field which is full of danger, full of snakes and pitfalls.

Q: Which means one has to be tremendously awake.

K: So I have learned from talking to him that this is a very dangerous thing. He has said you can only understand whether

Krishnamurti is speaking the truth if you are really prepared to walk in a field which is full of pitfalls. Is that right?

Q: Yes.

K: It is a field which is full of mines, the razor's edge path. Are you prepared to do that? One's whole being says "Be secure".

Q: That is the only way to do anything.

K: I have learnt to be aware of the dangers around me and also to face danger all the time and therefore to have no security. The enquirer might say, "This is too much" and go away!

So this is what I want to get at. Can the mind—which has been conditioned for centuries to be secure—abandon that, and say, "I will walk into danger"? That is what we are saying. It is logical, but in a sense it is illogical.

Q: In principle that is the way all science works.

K: Yes, that is right. So it also means I don't trust anybody—any guru, any prophet. I trust my wife because she loves me and I love her, but that is irrelevant.

Q: The word danger has to be explained too. From one point it is dangerous, and from another it isn't. I have to investigate. My conditioning is very dangerous.

K: So we're saying: "I have walked in danger and I have found the logic of this danger. Through the perception of the danger I have found the truth of what Krishnamurti is saying. And there is no security, no safety in this. Whereas all the others give me safety."

Q: Security becomes the ultimate danger.

K: Of course.

Q: What you have described is actually the scientific approach. They say every statement must be in danger of being false; it has been put that way.

K: That is perfectly right. I have learnt a lot—have you? A man comes from Seattle or Sheffield or Birmingham and is told: "I have found that what he says is the truth because I have had a perception and that perception stands logically". It is not outside of reason. And in that perception I see that where I walk is full of pitfalls, of danger. Therefore I have to be tremendously aware. Danger exists when there is no security. And the gurus, the priests, all offer security. Seeing the illogic of it I accept this illogic too.

Q: I am not sure that you should call it illogical; it is not illogical but it is the way logic has to work.

K: Of course. Are we saying that direct perception, insight and the working out of it demand great logic, a great capacity to think clearly? But the capacity to think clearly will not bring about insight.

Q: But if the logic does not bring about perception, what does it do exactly?

K: It trains, it sharpens the mind. But that certainly won't bring about an insight.

Q: It is not through the mind that the perception comes.

K: That all depends on what you mean by the mind. Logic makes the mind sharp, clear, objective and sane. But that won't give you the other. Your question is: How does the other come about?

Q (1): No. That was not my question. Logic clears the mind, but is the mind the instrument of perception?

Q (2): You see, you must have the perception. If you have a perception, for example, about the ending of sorrow, or fear, it may be that the whole thing is a deception. Logic is something which provides the clarity in what you are doing from there on.

Q (3): Yes, that is what we said, that it clears the mind of confusion, of the débris.

Q (4): The débris may come if you don't have logic.

K: You might remain in the débris if you don't have logic.

Q: If the perception is a real perception and so the truth, why does it then need the discipline of logic to examine it?

K: We said perception works out logically. It does not need logic. Whatever it does is reasonable, logical, sane, objective.

Q: It is logical without an intent to make it so.

K: That's it.

Q: It is like saying that if you see what is in this room correctly, you will not find anything illogical in what you see.

K: All right. Will the perception keep the confusion, the débris away all the time so that the mind never accumulates it and doesn't have to keep clearing it away? That was your question, wasn't it?

Q: I think perception can reach the stage at which it is continually keeping the field clear. I say that it can reach that stage for a certain moment.

K: At a certain moment I have perception. But during the interval between the perceptions there is a lot of débris being gathered. Our question is: Is perception continuous so that there is no collection of the débris? Put it round the other way: Does one perception keep the field clear?

Q: Can one make a difference between insight and perception?

K: Don't break it up yet. Take those two words as synonymous. We are asking: Is perception from time to time, with intervals? During those intervals a lot of débris collects and therefore the field has to be swept again. Or does perception in itself bring about tremendous clarity in which there is no débris?

Q: Are you saying that once it happens it will be there for ever?

K: That is what I am trying to get at. Don't use the words "continuous," "never again". Keep to the question: Once perception has taken place can the mind collect further débris, confusion? It is only when that perception becomes darkened by the débris, that the process of getting rid of it begins. But if there is perception why should there be a collecting, gathering?

Q: There are a lot of difficult points in this.

II

KRISHNAMURTI: We were discussing how one can know what Krishnamurti is saying is true. He might be caught in his own conditioning, illusions and knowing them, and not being able to free himself from them, have put together a series of observations, words, and call them truth. How do you know whether what he is saying is actual, truthful and lasting?

Dr Bohm said that when one has an insight, a direct perception into what is being said, then there is no doubt that it is the truth. Having that insight you can work it out logically to show that the perception is true. But is that perception brief, only to be had at intervals and therefore gathering a lot of débris—those things that block perception—or is *one* perception enough? Does it open the door so that there is insight all the time?

Q: Does that mean that you would never have any confusion?

K: Yes, we came to that point. One has a perception, an insight, and that insight has its own capacity for reason, logic and action. That action is complete, because the perception is complete for the moment. Will further action confuse perception? Or, having perception is there no further confusion?

Q: I think we were saying that there is danger in this. If you say: My action is always right . . .

K: Oh, that is dangerous!

Q: We also said that logic has its danger. One could think one has an insight when one has not.

K: Suppose I have the capacity to reason it out and act and then say: That is a perfect, complete action. Some people who read the *Gita* act according to it and they call that insight. Their action is patterned after their reading. They say this action is complete. I have heard many of them say this; also Catholics and Protestants who are completely immersed in the Bible. So we are treading on very dangerous ground and therefore are greatly aware of it.

Q: You also said that the mind tries to find security in all this.

K: The mind has always been seeking security and when that security is threatened it tries to find security in insight, in direct perception.

Q: In the illusion of insight.

K: Yes, but it makes the insight into security. The next question is: Must there be a constant breaking of perception? That is, one day one sees very clearly, one has direct perception, then that fades away and there is confusion. Then again there is a perception and an action, followed by confusion and so on. Is that so? Or is there no further confusion after these deep insights?

Q: Are we saying this perception is whole?

K: Yes, if the perception is complete, whole, then there is no confusion at any time. Or, one may deceive oneself that it is whole and act upon it, which brings confusion.

Q: There is also a possible danger that one has a genuine perception, an insight, and is not fooling oneself and that out of that comes a certain action. But then one could fall into making whatever that action was into a formula and stop having the insight. Let's say that out of an insight which was real a certain action came. One then thinks that is the way things should be.

K: That is what generally happens.

Q: But isn't that a corruption of the perception, just making a pattern out of the action instead of continuing to look? It is like being able to really look at something, for instance looking out of the window and something is seen. But then you don't look out again and think everything is the way it was. It may have totally changed. The perception starts out being genuine, but you don't continue to look, have insight.

K: Yes. Scientists may have an insight in some specialized field and that insight is put into a category of science unrelated to their life. But we are talking of a perception that is not only in the field of action but also in daily life.

Q: As a whole and so there is a continuity.

K: Yes.

Q: But I still don't think we have gone into the question of danger. You said that one day a man came to you and said maybe you were stuck in a groove.

K: Yes, caught in a rut.

Q: You didn't say immediately, "I know I am not because I have had a perfect insight."

K: Ah, that would be deadly!

Q: But rather, you said you looked at it for several days.

K: Of course.

Q: I am trying to find out what we are driving at. Perhaps we are saying that there *may* be an insight which never goes back into confusion. But we are not saying there *is* one.

K: Yes, that's right. Now would you say, when there is complete perception—not an illusory perception—there is no further confusion?

Q: It seems reasonable to say that.

K: That means from day to day there is no confusion at all.

Q: Then why did you feel it necessary to look into it?

K: Because I may deceive myself. Therefore it is dangerous ground and I must be alert, I must watch it.

Q: Are we seeing this as an insight now?—that when there is an insight of that kind there is no further confusion? But we may deceive ourselves nevertheless.

K: Yes. Therefore we must be watchful.

Q: Do you mean after the real insight you could then deceive yourself?

K: No. You have a deep insight, complete, whole. Someone comes along and says: "Look, you are deceiving yourself." Do you instantly say, "No, I am not deceiving myself because my perception was complete"? Or do you listen and look at it all afresh? It doesn't mean that you are denying the complete perception, you are again watching if it is real or illusory.

Q: That is not necessarily an intellectual process?

K: No, no. I would say both. It is intellectual as well as non-verbal.

Q: Is perception something that is always there and it is only that we . . .

K: That leads to dangerous ground. The Hindus say that God is always there inside you—the abiding deep divinity, or soul, or Atman, and it is covered up. Remove the confusion, the débris and it is found inside. Most people believe that. I think that is a conclusion. You conclude that there is something divine inside, a soul, the Atman or whatever you like to call it. And from a conclusion you can never have a total, complete perception.

Q: But this leads to another problem, because if you deny that, then what makes one step out of the stream? Does it mean that the stepping out is for certain individuals only?

K: When you say "certain individuals" I think you are putting the wrong question, aren't you?

Q: No. If the possibility exists for everyone . . .

K: Yes, the possibility exists for human beings.

Q: For the totality?

K: For human beings.

Q: Then there is some energy which . . .

K: Which is outside of them or which is in them.

Q: Yes. We don't know.

K: Therefore don't come to any conclusion. If from a conclusion you think you perceive, then that perception is conditioned, therefore it is not whole.

Q: Does that mean that there would not be the possibility of a deepening of perception?

K: You can't deepen insight. You can't deepen perception. You perceive the whole—that's all.

Q: What do you mean then by saying there was this mind into which you could continually go more deeply?

K: That is something else.

Q: Are you saying that perception, if it is partial, is not perception?

K: Of course, obviously not.

Q (1): So the deepening of perception would only be a partial step. That wouldn't be perception.

Q (2): You mentioned watchfulness after perception.

K: What happened was: A man came up to me and said, "You are getting old, you are stuck in a groove." And I listened to it. For a couple of days I thought about it. I looked at it and said to myself, "He may be right."

Q: You are almost suggesting that it could be possible.

K: No, I wanted to examine it. Don't say it could, or could not.

Q: I was going to ask: to be caught in habit after a perception, could that not ever happen again, at certain levels?

K: There is partial perception and total perception—let's divide it into those two. When there is total perception there is no further confusion.

Q: You don't get caught in habit?

K: There is no further confusion. Because it is so.

Q: What if something happens to the brain physically?

K: Then of course it is gone.

Q: So there seems to be a limitation to what you say, because one assumes that the brain remains healthy.

K: Of course, assuming that the whole organism is healthy. If there is an accident, your brain suffers concussion and something is injured, then it is finished.

Q (1): The major danger is that we would mistake a partial perception for the total.

Q (2): But it still means that it is "here". You are not tapping it from "out there". That energy is within you, isn't it?

K: One has to go into this question of what is perception. How do you come to it? That is very important, isn't it? You cannot have perception if your daily life is in disorder, confused, contradictory. That is obvious.

Q: Doesn't this perception mean that there is constant renewal?

K: No. Is that energy outside, or inside? She is asking that question all the time.

Q: Isn't that an artificial division: Outside and inside? Is that a real thing, or is it just an illusion?

K: She said that this perception needs energy. That energy may be an external energy, a mechanical energy, or a non-mechanistic energy which may exist deeply inside you. Both are mental concepts. Would you agree to that? Both are conclusions which one has either accepted because tradition has said so, or one has come to that conclusion by oneself. Any form of conclusion is detrimental to perception. So what does perception mean? Can I have perception if I am attached to my position, to my wife, to my property?

Q: It colours the act of perceiving.

K: Yes, but take the scientists, they have their family, their attachments, they want a position, money and all the rest of it, but they have an insight.

Q: It is not total.

K: So we are saying that total perception can only take place when in your daily life there is no confusion.

Q: May we look more closely into that, because couldn't it be that a total perception can take place in spite of that and wipe it away?

K: I can see if the windows are not clean my view is confused.

Q: Would that mean that there is a conditioned insight?

K: If I am in fear my perception will be very partial. That is a fact.

Q: But don't you need perception to end fear?

K: Ah, but in investigating fear I have a total perception of fear.

Q: Surely if there is fear, or attachment, even one's logic would be distorted.

K: One is frightened—as we said, that distorts perception. But in investigating, observing, going into fear, understanding it profoundly, in delving into it I have perception.

Q: Are you implying that there are certain things you can do which will make for perceptions? Which means although you have fear and it distorts, the distortion is not so total that you cannot investigate it. There is still that possibility, although you are distorting through fear?

K: I realize I am distorting perception through fear.

Q: That's right, then I begin to look at fear.

K: Investigate it, look into it.

Q: In the beginning I am also distorting it.

K: Therefore I am watching every distortion. I am aware of every distortion that is going on.

Q: But you see, I think the difficulty lies there. How can I investigate when I am distorting?

K: Wait, just listen. I am afraid and I see fear has made me do something which is a distortion.

Q: But before I can see that, the fear has to fade away.

K: No, I am observing fear.

Q (1): But I cannot observe fear if I am afraid.

Q (2): How can you observe it if you are *not* afraid?

Q (3): What is it that is observing?

K: Take a fact: you are afraid. You are conscious of it. That means that you become aware of the fact that there is fear. And you observe also what that fear has done. Is that clear?

Q: Yes.

K: And you look more and more into it. In looking very deeply into it you have an insight.

Q: I may have an insight.

K: No, you *will* have insight, which is quite different.

Q: What you are saying is that this confusion due to fear is not complete, that it is always open to mankind to have insight.

K: To one who is investigating, who is observing.

Q: If you try to investigate something else while you are afraid you get lost in fear. But it is still open to you to investigate fear.

K: Yes, quite right. One suffers and you see what it does. In observing it, investigating it, opening it up, in the very unrolling of it you have a certain insight. That is all we are saying. That insight may be partial. Therefore one has to be aware that it is partial. Its action is partial and it may appear complete, so watch it.

Q: Very often it looks as if it is totally impossible to have an insight, since you say: "If you are distorting how will you look?" But you are also saying, that as a matter of fact, when you have a distortion, the one thing you can look at is the distortion.

K: That's right.

Q: That factually you have that capacity.

K: One *has* that capacity.

239

Q (1): So when you are distorting something through fear or suffering, most things you look at will be distorted. But it is actually possible to look at that distortion itself.

Q (2): You can look at *that*. The fear which creates the distortion can be looked at; so you can't say that no perception whatsoever is possible.

K: That's just it. Then you have locked the door.

Q: Could one say that the fear can look at itself?

K: No, no. One is afraid: in looking at that fear—not having an insight, just watching it—you see what it does, what its action is.

Q: You mean by looking, being aware of it.

K: Without any choosing—being aware. And you see what fear does. In looking at it more extensively, deeply, widely, suddenly you have an insight into the whole structure of fear.

Q: But there is still the question: in that moment of fear, I *am* fear.

K: How you observe fear matters—whether you observe it as an observer, or the observer is *that*. You perceive the observer is the observed and in this action there is distortion, confusion. And you examine that confusion, which is born of fear and in the very process of examination you have an insight. Do it, you will see it—if you don't limit yourself. In saying, "I am too frightened, I can't look", you run away from it.

Q: To simplify it perhaps too much: when we said one can't see through the window because it is dirty, it distorts, the action of examining the fear, the distorting factor, is the cleansing of the window.

K: How you observe, how you investigate, that is the real thing. That is, perception can only take place when there is no division between the observer and the observed. Perception can only take place in the very act of exploring: to explore implies there is no division between the observer and the observed. Therefore you are watching the movement of fear and in the very watching of it there is an insight. I think that is clear. And yet you see, Krishnamurti says: "I have never done this."

Q: Never gone through all this? Then how do you know somebody else can?

240

K: That's just it. Let's discuss it. Suppose you have not gone through all this, but you see it instantly. Because you see it instantly your capacity to reason explains all this. Another listens and says, "I'd like to get that, I don't have to go through that whole process."

Q: Are you saying that all we have been discussing just now is merely a pointer to something else? We don't have to go through all that.

K: Yes. I want to get at that.

Q: In other words, that helps to clear the ground in some way?

K: Yes.

Q: It is not really the main point.

K: No.

Q: Are you saying there is a short cut?

K: No, no short cut. Must you go through fear, jealousy, anxiety, attachment? Or can you clear the whole thing instantly? Must one go through all this process?

Q: You previously said that you have never done this. And by having that immediate total perception you are able to see what those with the dirty windows can do to clean them. But that isn't necessary, there is perhaps a direct, an immediate way for those who haven't . . .

K: No. First put the question, see what comes out of it.

Dr Bohm says to Krishnamurti: "You have probably not gone through all this. Because you have a direct, a total insight you can argue with reason, with logic; you can act. You are always talking from that total perception, therefore what you say can never be distorted." And another listens to all this and says: "I am frightened, I am jealous, I am this, I am that, and therefore I can't have total perception." So I observe attachment, or fear, or jealousy and I have an insight.

Is it possible through investigating, through awareness and discovering that the observer is the observed and that there is no division, in the very process of investigation—in which we are observing without the observer and see the totality of it—to free all the rest? I think that is the only way.

Q: Is it possible not to have certain fears, jealousy, attachment?

Could that be part of one's conditioning if one were raised in a certain way, or went to a certain school?

K: But there may be deeper layers. You may not be totally conscious of them, you may not be totally aware of the deeper fears, etc. You may say, superficially I am all right, I have none of these things.

Q: But if one went to a certain school, the kind of learning and investigation that would take place in such a school, would that clear the way towards the possibility?

K: Obviously. What we are talking about is: Must one go through all this process?

Q: Couldn't we remove from the problem the personal aspect? We are discussing what is open to man rather than to any individual.

K: Yes. Is it open to any human being without going through all this process?

Q: By "this process" do you mean involvement with the fear?

K: With fear, sorrow, jealousy, attachment, you go through all that, step by step. Or can a human being see the whole thing at a glance? And that very glance is the investigation and the complete, total perception.

Q: Which is what you mean when you say the first step is the last.

K: Yes, total perception.

Q: Then what would one's responsibility be towards someone who is in sorrow?

K: The response to that human being is the response of compassion. That's all. Nothing else.

Q: For instance, if you see an injured bird it is very easy to deal with that because it really doesn't require very much of you. But when you come in contact with a human being, he has a much more complex set of needs.

K: What can you do actually? Somebody comes to you and says, "I am in deep sorrow". Do you talk to him out of compassion, or from a conclusion, or out of your own particular experience of sorrow which has conditioned you, and you answer him according to your conditioning? A Hindu, who is conditioned in a certain way says: "My dear friend, I am so sorry, but in the next life you will live better. You suffered because you did this and that"—and so on. Or a Christian would respond from some other conclusion. And he takes comfort in it. Because a man who is suffering wants some sort of solace, someone on whose lap he can put his head. So what he is seeking is comfort and avoidance of this terrible pain. Will you offer him any of those escapes? Whatever comes out of compassion will help him.

Q: Are you saying that as far as sorrow is concerned you can't directly help anyone, but the energy of compassion itself may be of help?

K: That's right; that's all.

Q: But many such wounded spirits will come to the Centre here and I think it is going to be a problem to know how to deal with them.

K: There is no problem if you are compassionate. Compassion doesn't create problems. It has no problems, therefore it is compassionate.

Q: You are saying that total compassion is the highest intelligence?

K: Of course. If there is compassion, that compassion has its own intelligence and that intelligence acts. But if you have no compassion and no intelligence, then your conditioning makes you reply whatever he wants. I think that is fairly simple.

To go back to the other question: Must a human being go through the whole process? Has no human being said, "I won't go through all this. I absolutely refuse to go through all this"?

Q: But on what basis does one refuse? It wouldn't make sense to refuse to do what is necessary.

K: Of course. You see, we are such creatures of habit. Because my father is conditioned, generations after generations are conditioned and I am conditioned. And I accept it, I work in it and I operate with it. But if I say, I won't ever operate in my conditioned responses, something else may take place. Then, if I realize I am a bourgeois, I don't want to become an aristocrat or a militant, I refuse to be a bourgeois. Which doesn't mean I become a revolutionary, or join Lenin or Marx—those are all bourgeois to me. So something does take place. I reject the whole thing. You see, a human being never says, "I will reject the whole thing". I want to investigate that.

Q: Do you mean that even to say: "I am going to get rid of the whole thing" is not necessary?

K: Of course. I mean saying, "I won't be a bourgeois" is just words.

Q: But isn't the key to this somewhere in desire? There is some sort of desire for continuity, for security.

K: That's right. Bourgeois implies continuity, security, it implies belonging to something, a lack of taste, vulgarity—all that.

Q: But Krishnaji, if you are saying that Krishnamurti never said this, never had the need to say it, we can only conclude that you are some kind of freak.

K: No, no. You can say he is a freak but it doesn't answer the question. Krishnamurti says, "I have not touched all this". Somebody asks, "Why should I go through all this?" Don't say Krishnamurti is a freak, but ask: "How does it happen?"

Q: In saying, "I won't be a bourgeois" you are discovering it in yourself.

K: No, no. That is a different matter. If somebody says to you, "I have never been through all this", what do you do? Do you say he is a freak? Or would you say: "How extraordinary, is he telling the truth? Has he deceived himself?" You discuss with him. Then your question is: "How does it happen?" You are a human being, he is a human being: you want to find out.

Q: You ask: "In what way are we different?" He is a human being that has never been through all that, and yet he points out.

K: No, he has never been through it. Don't say he points out. Don't you ask that question: "How does it happen, must I go through all this?" Do you ask that?

Q (1): I have assumed I must.

Q (2): Krishnaji, you are taking two widely separate things. One is the uncontaminated person, who never had to go through the process because he was never in the soup.

K: Leave out why he didn't go through it.

Q: But most other people, apparently, are in some form of . . .

244

K: ... conditioning ...

Q (1): ... in some form of contamination, it may be fear, or something else. Therefore the person who has already got this sickness—let's call it that—says, "This man has never been sick for a day in his life." What good is it to examine that, because one is already sick in some form.

Q (2): That is an assumption. I think we are saying that if any one human being never went through all this, that says something about the essence of mankind, which is a truth for everybody.

Q (3): But one is already sick.

Q (4): That may be a conclusion.

Q (5): It is also an ascertainable fact.

Q (6): I think one is assuming that whatever this sickness is, it is in the essence, it is essentially inevitable.

Q (7): I didn't say that. But I am saying it is a fact—at least it is to me—that there is the sickness in some form or another. I don't think that is an assumption. I think that is a fact.

Q (8): But the question is: What does the fact depend upon? You see, the fact may depend upon an assumption which people make about themselves that it will take time to overcome that sickness.

Q (9): Is it part of the sickness to ask only about small things and not the greater things?

Q (10): Aside from all that the question is: How can a human being who is sick in some way, how can he get out of it directly without going through endless self-exploration?

K: Can we put the whole thing differently? Do you seek excellence, not excellence for instance in a building, but the essence of excellence? Then everything falls away, doesn't it? Or do you seek excellence in a certain direction and never the essence of excellence? As an artist I seek excellence in my painting and get caught in that. A scientist gets caught in something else. But an ordinary human being, not a specialist, just an average intelligent human being who does not take drugs, does not smoke, is fairly intelligent and decent, if he sought the essence of excellence, would this happen? The essence would meet all this. I wonder if I am conveying something?

Q: Does it exist apart from this manifestation?

K: Listen carefully first. Don't object, or reject and say "if" and "but". That very demand for excellence—how you demand it—brings the essence of it. You demand it passionately. You demand the highest intelligence, the highest excellence, the essence of it, and when fear arises, then you . . .

Q: Where does the demand come from?

K: *Demand* it! Don't say: "Where does it come from?" There may be a motive, but the very demand washes it all away. I wonder if I am conveying anything?

Q: You are saying: Demand this excellence—which we don't know.

K: I don't know what is beyond it, but I want to be morally excellent.

Q: Does that mean goodness?

K: I demand the excellence of goodness, I demand the excellent flower of goodness. In that very demand there is a demand for the essence.

Q: Does perception come from this demand?

K: Yes, that's right.

Q: Could you go into what you call this demand?

K: It is not a demand which means asking, a demand that means imploring, wanting—cut out all those.

Q: It doesn't mean those?

K: No, no.

Q: But then you are back with prayer.

K: Oh, no. Leave out all that.

Q: You are really saying that the impossible is possible to the average intelligent human being?

K: We are saying that, yes. Which is not a conclusion, which is not a hope. I say it is possible for the average human being, who is fairly clean, who is fairly decent, fairly kind, who is not a bourgeois.

Q: Traditionally we are conditioned to believe that there are special people with no conscious content of consciousness, so it is very difficult for someone like me to feel that one could really be completely free of it.

K: You see, you have not listened. X says to you: "Please listen first, don't bring in all these objections. Just listen to what he is saying. That is, what is important in life is the supreme excellence which has its own essence." That's all. And to demand does not mean begging or praying, getting something from somebody.

Q: The point is, we find we confuse demand with desire.

K: Of course.

Q: There must be no beliefs.

K: No beliefs, no desire.

Q: You see, when people feel that they want to give up desire then there is a danger of giving up this demand as well.

K: How can we put this? Let's find a good word for it. Would the word "passion" be suitable? There is passion for this, passion for excellence.

Q: Does it imply that this passion has no object?

K: You see how you immediately form a conclusion. Burning passion—not *for* something. The Communists are passionate about their ideas. That passion is very, very petty and limited. The Christians have passion for missionary work—that passion is born of the love of Jesus. That again is not passion, it is very narrow. Putting all that aside, I say: "Passion".

Q: As you were just saying, people have had some vision, or a dream of something and that has developed a great energy. But you are saying it is not a dream, it is not a vision; but it is nevertheless some perception of this excellence.

K: All those passions feed the ego, feed the me, make me important, consciously or unconsciously. We are cutting out all that.

There is a young boy who has a passion to grow up into an extraordinary human being, into something original.

Q: He sees that it is possible.

K: Yes.

Q: And therefore he has the passion.

K: Yes, that's right. It is possible. Is that what is missing in most human beings? Not passion, but the welling up of ... I don't know how to put it. There is this passion in a human being who demands the supreme excellence, not in what he writes in his books, but the *feeling* of it. You know this, don't you?—that may shatter everything else. Again, that human being didn't demand it. He says: "I never even asked for it."

Q: Perhaps that is due to conditioning. We are conditioned to mediocrity, not to make this demand. That is what you mean by mediocrity.

K: Yes, of course. Mediocrity is lack of great passion—not for Jesus, or for Marx or whatever it is.

Q: We are not only conditioned to mediocrity but to direction, so the demand is always to have some direction.

K: The demand is a direction, quite right.

Q: To have a demand without any direction . . .

K: That's right. I like the word "demand", because it is a challenge.

Q: Doesn't a demand without direction imply that it is not in time?

K: Of course. It demands no direction, no time, no person. So does total insight bring this passion? Total insight *is* the passion.

Q: They can't be separate.

K: Total insight is the flame of passion which wipes away all confusion. It burns away everything else. Don't you then act as a magnet? The bees go towards the nectar. In the same way don't you act as a magnet when you are passionate to create? Is it that there is this lack of fire? That may be the thing that is missing. If there is something missing I would ask for it.

Q (1): Could we talk about the relationship between the conditioned and the unconditioned mind, and whether it is only possible to ask for small things, or can we somehow leap beyond that into something bigger?

Q (2): Whatever the me asks for, the asking in a direction *is* the small thing.

K: Quite right.

Q: We have to ask for the unlimited, for the unconditioned.

K: She is really asking: What is the relationship between the conditioned and the unconditioned? Also, what is the relationship between two human beings, when one is unconditioned and the other is not? There is no relationship.

Q: How can you say that there is no relationship between the unconditioned and the conditioned human being?

K: There is no relationship from the conditioned to the unconditioned. But the unconditioned has a relationship to the other.

Q: But logically one could ask: Is there an essential difference between the unconditioned and the conditioned? Because if you say there is, then there is duality.

K: What do you mean by essential difference?

Q: Let's say difference in kind. If there is an essential difference between the conditioned and the unconditioned there is duality.

K: I see what you mean. X is conditioned, Y is not conditioned. X thinks in terms of duality, his very conditioning is duality. But duality has no relationship with Y, yet Y has a relationship to X.

Q: Because there is no duality.

K: Yes. Y has no duality therefore there is a relationship.
   You also asked some other question: Essentially, deeply, is there a difference? Are not both the same?

Q: Could one ask the question in another way? Is the conditioning only superficial?

K: No. Then we are lost.

Q (1): Could we put it like this? When you say, "You are the world, the world is you"—does that statement include the conditioned as well as the unconditioned?

Q (2): I am not sure about that. It seems that if the unconditioned mind can be related to the conditioned, can understand the conditioned, comprehend it, then there is not really a duality, that is fundamentally, in essence. The unconditioned mind comprehends the conditioned mind and goes beyond it.

Q (3): The world couldn't be unconditioned, could it?

K: The world is 'me' and 'me' is the world.

Q: That is an absolute fact only to the unconditioned.

K: Oh, not at all. Be careful, it is so. It is an obvious fact.

Q: You mean that only the unconditioned can perceive that?

K: That is what she says. I am refuting it. I say it isn't quite like that.

Q: I mean it in the sense that I may say, "I am the world, the world is me", but I revert to an action which is a contradiction to that. Therefore it is not an absolute fact for me. There may be moments when the fact of it is seen by me.

K: Yes. Do you mean: "I say to myself very clearly, 'I am the world and the world is me' "?

Q: I see it.

K: I feel it.

Q: I feel it, yes.

K: And I act contrary to that. Which is, I act personally, selfishly—my, me. That is a contradiction to the fact that the world is me and I am the world. A person can say this merely as an intellectual conclusion, or a momentary feeling.

Q: It is not an intellectual conclusion, because I am stating my position, but I accept that for you the position is totally different.

K: No, you don't even have to accept that. See the fact, which is, when one says, "I am the world and the world is me" there is no me. But one's house has to be insured. I may have children, I have to earn a living—but there is no me. See the importance of it. There is no me all the time. I function, but there is no me which is seeking a higher position and all that. Though I am married I am not attached, I don't depend on a wife or husband. The appearances may give you the impression that the me is operating, but actually to a man who feels, "The world is me and I am the world", to him there is no me. To you, looking at him, there is. That human being lives in this world, he must have food, clothes and shelter, a job, transportation, all that, yet there is no me.

So when the world is me and I am the world, there is no me. Can that state, that quality operate in all directions? It *must* operate in all directions. When you say, "I am the world and the world is me", and there is no me, there is no conditioning. I don't put the question: In that unconditioned state does the conditioned exist? When a human being says, "I am the world and the world is me", there is no I.

Q: Therefore the other person also is not there. There is no you.

K: There is no me, there is no you. When you ask if the conditioned exists in this state you are asking a wrong question. That is what I was getting at. Because when there is no I there is no you.

Q: The question is: How does that person see the kind of confusion that arises around I and you. He sees what is going on in the world, that people are generally confused about this.

K: I exist: there is you and me. And you also think the same thing. So we keep this division everlastingly. But when you and I really realize, have profound insight that, "The world is me and I am the world", there is no me.

Q: There is no me and no you. "No" means "everything".

K: The world of living—everything.

Q: Then the question, "Is there an essential difference between this and that, the unconditioned and the conditioned", doesn't arise, because there is no "between".

K: Yes, that's right. There is no you, there is no I in that state, which doesn't include the conditioned state. Is this too abstract?

Q: Why do you have to say, "I am the world" first, and then deny this?

K: Because it is an actuality.

Q: But then you imply that the I is still there if I say, "I am the world".

K: That is merely a statement. It is an actual fact that I am the world.

Q: Whatever I mean by the word "I", I also mean by the word "world".

K: Yes.

Q: So we don't need those two words.

K: Yes. You and I—remove that.

Q: There is just everything.

K: No, this is very dangerous. If you say I am everything . . .

Q: I am trying to find out what you mean by "the world".

K: If you say, "I am everything", then the murderer, the assassin is part of me.

Q: Suppose I say, "I am the world" instead, does that change it?

K: (*laughing*) All right. I see the actual fact that I am the result of the world. The world means killing, wars, the whole of society—I am the result of that.

Q: And I see everybody is the result of that.

K: Yes. I am saying the result is I and you.

Q: And that separation.

K: When I say I am the world, I am saying all that.

Q: You mean to say I am generated by the world, I am identified with everything.

K: Yes. I am the product of the world

Q: The world is the essence of what I am.

K: Yes. I am the essence of the world. It is the same thing. When there is a deep perception of that, not verbal, not intellectual, not emotional, not romantic, but profound, there is no you or me. I think that holds logically. But there is a danger. If I say the world is me, I am everything, I'll accept everything.

Q: You are really saying that one is the product of the whole of society.

K: Yes.

Q: But I am also of the essence of the whole of society.

K: Yes. I am really the essential result of all this.

Q: Does it help to use the word "ego"?

K: It is the same thing, it doesn't matter. You see, when you say me, or ego, there is a possibility of deception that 'I' is the very essence of God. You know about that superstition.

Q: The Atman.

K: Yes.

Q: But there is still another question. Is the unconditioned mind also a product of all this? Then we come to a contradiction.

K: No, there is no contradiction. Without using the word "I" it can be said: the result of the world is *this*. The result of the world is *that* also. We are two human beings, which means the result has created the I and the you. When there is an insight into the result there is no "result".

Q: The result changes and vanishes when we see it.

K: That means there is no result. Therefore 'you' and 'I' don't exist. That is an actual fact for a man who says, "I am not the result". You see what it means? There is no causation in the mind and therefore there is no effect. Therefore it is whole, and any action born of it is causeless and without effect.

Q: You have to make that clear, in the sense that you still use cause and effect concerning ordinary, mechanical things.

K: Quite. This human being, X, is a result. And Y is a result. X says I, and Y says I; therefore there is you and I. X says I see this and investigates, goes into it and he has an insight. In that insight the two results cease. Therefore in that state there is no cause.

Q: There is no cause and no effect although it may leave a residue in the mind.

K: Let's go into it. In that state there is no result, no cause, no effect. That mind acts out of compassion. Therefore there is no result.

Q: But in some sense it would look as if there were a result.

K: But compassion has no result. A is suffering, he says to X, "Please help me to get out of my suffering." If X really has compassion his words have no result.

Q: Something happens, but there is no result.

K: That's it.

Q: But I think people generally are seeking a result.

K: Yes. Let's put it another way. Does compassion have a result? When there is result there is cause. When compassion has a cause then you are no longer compassionate.

Q (1): It is an extremely subtle thing, because something happens which seems final and yet it is not.

Q (2): But compassion also acts.

K: Compassion is compassion, it doesn't act. If it acts because there is a cause and an effect, then it is not compassion: it wants a result.

Q: It acts purely.

K: It wants a result.

Q: What makes it want a result is the idea of separation. Somebody says, "There is a person suffering, I would like to produce the result that he is not suffering." But that is based on the idea that there is me and he.

K: That's it.

Q: There is no he and no I. There is no room, no place to have this result.

K: It is a tremendous thing! One has to look at it very, very carefully. Look, "The world is me and I am the world". When I say me, you exist: both of us are there. The you and the I are the results of man's misery, of selfishness, and so on—it is a result. When one looks into the result, goes into it very, very deeply, the insight brings about a quality in which you and I—who are the result—don't exist. This is easy to agree to verbally, but when you see it deeply there is no you and no me. Therefore there is no result—which means compassion. The person upon whom that compassion acts wants a result. We say, "Sorry, there is no result." But the man who suffers says, "Help me to get out of this", or, "Help me to bring back my son, my wife", or whatever it is. He is demanding a result. This thing has no result. The result is the world.

Q: Does compassion affect the consciousness of man?

K: Yes. It affects the deep layers of consciousness.

The I is the result of the world, the you is the result of the world. And to the man who sees this deeply with a profound insight, there is no you or I. Therefore that profound insight is compassion—which is intelligence. And the intelligence says: If you want a result I can't give it to you, I am not the product of a result. Compassion says: This state is not a result, therefore there is no cause.

Q: Does that mean there is no time either?

K: No cause, no result, no time.